Zdeněk Kratochvíl

The Philosophy
of Living Nature

Translated by Václav Paris

KAROLINUM PRESS
PRAGUE 2016

KAROLINUM PRESS
Karolinum Press is the publishing department of Charles University in Prague
Ovocný trh 3, 116 36 Prague 1
Czech Republic
www.karolinum.cz

Designed by Jan Šerých
Set and printed in the Czech Republic by Karolinum Press

Cataloging-in-Publication Data is available from the National Library
of the Czech Republic

ISBN 978-80-246-3131-8
ISBN 978-80-246-3133-2 (pdf)

Contents

1. The philosophical concept of nature—*physis.* The traditionally problematic quality of natural philosophy. The decline and resurgence of a sense for *physis*

Our aim is to think about nature philosophically. Thinking philosophically means thinking for wisdom, and not for a particular end. For the European conception of philosophy it also means developing a conceptual language. How can conceptual language contribute to wisdom? Only by gradually revealing that which is shown to be properly thinkable. In European philosophy we call this revelation of the thinkable "truth," originally the Greek *aletheia*, that is, the situation when *lethe* (concealing, forgetting) is not omnipotent because it yields to thought. But are living nature and the natural so entirely transparent to thought—at least to thought that strives after wisdom? Can the experience of nature and natural experience be translated into a conceptual system of true statements? The scope of this question will only gradually become clear to us. Often we will have to be less ambitious, and instead of searching for and investigating the truth of nature, we'll have to search for and investigate the relationship between natural experience and conceptual knowledge. Our allegedly "natural" experience is always already somehow pre-formed by some structure of thought, thanks to which we perceive the experience in a certain way and can express it in words. But is a conceptual disclosure of truth the only route that a rationally ordered discussion can take when it leads its battle for sense in the name of wisdom?

In everyday speech we believe that we know what we mean when we use the words "nature" and "natural." In the most informal sense of the word, nature is what we see around us when we take a daytrip beyond the city boundaries. It may have been despoiled, but it's still green in places. Everything unnatural is damaging to nature—everything technological, and this harms us as well (our nature) although we are willing to go about our daily work in the frame of such technology because of its results. For this reason it is often said that we are estranged from nature. Are we then estranged even from our own nature? And what kind of nature is that? Could correct hygiene (that is, different technology) help remedy our inner nature, just as ecological activities (again different technology) can remedy damaged nature outside?

We also have an array of sciences about nature: from physics and astronomy, through geology and chemistry to biology. Each of these sciences possesses a wide-ranging conceptual apparatus for describing a large experimental experience of certain properties of something in nature. Each of them describes a different side of nature, looks for a functional model of different classes of phenomena. Notably physics (the most general), astronomy (the most holistic and oldest, the most "cosmic"), and biology (penetrating into the most "natural," into the secret of life) all exist in a traditional symbiosis (or strife) with philosophy. Aren't we too bold, then, in wanting to philosophize about something, around which there are so many, so well established sciences? We are too used to the idea that philosophy thrives wherever there is a lack of knowledge. But even this idea holds some water, for traditionally philosophy grew from wonder, including wonder at the as yet unknown. Nevertheless, reasonable philosophers tend to have respect for the natural sciences; they stress that the concern of philosophy is *being* itself and that the perspective of philosophic exploration is essence *per se* and not a particular view of it. This is already stated in the customary definition (Aristotle's) of "first philosophy," ontology (of being *qua* being). Here lies the secret of philosophy; philosophy is inherently undisturbed by any science on the same subject, if only because what it concerns itself with is not a mere subject. Should the philosopher not then rather ask the physicist what he knows of *physis*; the astronomer what the cosmos is; the chemist what matter is; biologist what life is, and then to generalize it to the highest degree and thus create the philosophy of nature? We regard attempts undertaken in this direction as so formidable, that it would be unfair to cite them.

Scientists really do know a lot, but what they know usually differs slightly from what interests the common man, and differs yet more from what is aimed at by the philosophical question. The question regarding the natural is a philosophical one. It is, in fact, one of the oldest philosophical questions. It's at least as old, if not older than the word "philosophy" itself. The writings of the fifth and sixth century BC. Greek sages—the works of the pre-Socratics—tend on the whole to be given the same title by the authors of later antiquity: *Peri physeos*, *On Nature*. The starting points of philosophy are slowly established with these thinkers, and their fragmentary writings testify to a great attempt at thinking about nature. This attempt can be labeled as the widest-ranging protophilosophy, one in many ways far more substantial than the later systems of the metaphysical schools. It is precisely the unrepeatability of Anaximander's, Heraclitus', Empedocles', and Anaxagoras' cogitations that has prevented us from appropriating the title given to them, *Peri physeos*. But what happened to nature and the natural after we first rejected it as beneath us (during the Middle Ages), and then tried to press-gang it into our service, refashioning it in the image of our needs?

For the purposes of orientation, let us begin our return with an exploration of the meanings of words. Although etymology itself is not a source of philosophical knowledge—merely reflecting human linguistic traditions, it can alert us to certain connections, the relevance of which it will then become necessary to explore. Thus, the Czech word for "nature" ["*příroda*"] is allegedly very old, originally denoting "what was added by birth, the co-growth" ["*co se přirodilo, přírůstek*"] and later also "what comes to be without the interference of humankind" ["*co vzniká bez zásahu člověka*"]. Thus the natural is that which goes with birth, what belongs "to nature" and not in the sphere of the man-made or thought-up. Should we wish to abandon our dependence solely on our mother tongue, we can help ourselves with a detour through the mother tongue of philosophy, via the Greek word *physis*.

Physis is one of the oldest words in Greek. The first usage appears already in Homer, at least if the instance in question (*Odyssey* 10.303) is genuine. It would seem therefore, that *with physis* we are dealing with a pre-philosophic word. It is the post-verbal of the verb *phyomai*, which in this middle voice means "I am born." Thus *physis* is the "innate nature" of a thing. (Renaissance Czech translated *physis* yet more directly as "*přirození*" ["with birthing"], that is, until this Old Czech word became a euphemism for the sexual organs. But even then, the semantic shift still stressed a particular connotation of *physis*: a sign of nature is fertility, and *physis* points towards intimacy, spontaneity, and the power of transience.) In the Homeric epics and elsewhere, however, we usually meet *physis* in its verbal forms, alongside *phyomai* also the active *phyo*: "I give birth, I grow, I flower." In this way, of course, the word *physis* takes on many further meanings as well (similarly to the later *phye*, a different derivation of the same word): "growth," "likeness," "aspect," "essence," or "living being." Generally then, it connects on the one hand to origins and the embryonic, and on the other to the act of distinguishing according to appearance. Surprisingly, even for the ancient Greeks, *physis* was the opposite of the city and its built-up surroundings, albeit differently than it is for us. *Physis* is "wild," rugged, "virgin nature," which wakes dread even in the midst of her beauty. It is the preserve of the goddess Artemis, the harsh maiden, beautiful provider and hunter of all that is natural, unmade and untamed. Artemis is the godly dimension of *physis*.

Indo-European linguistic associations can point yet further into the past. The Indo-European *bhu-* corresponds to the Greek root *"phy-"*. And often accompanying this root in Indo-European languages are significations that range between being and plants. Consider for example the Vedic *bhuti*, "strength, success, riches"; in Czech *"býti"* ["to be"], in Greek *phyton* (perhaps *puta* in Mycenaean), meaning "plant." What is concerned is a relation to the power of being, which is perceived either vegetatively or generatively.

Another important point for the history of ideas was the Latin translation of the Greek expression *physis* using the word *natura*, or "that which belongs to birthing; has been born; moves towards birth." For a long time this word preserved the semantic range of the Greek expression *physis*. (The Old Czech translation as *"přirození"* provides evidence of this, for in the Czech conversational borrowing of the word *natura*, we read correctly another meaning present in the Greek *physis*: "disposition, constitution, the character of a living being.") Despite these facts, there is one essential, albeit indirect, difference between the Latin word *natura* and the Greek word *physis*. It results from later Latin opposing the adjective *naturalis* with the word *supernaturalis*—"above nature, supernatural." This concept was often used by Latin speaking Christians, yet for reasons other than merely linguistic ones, it is possible to conclude that it comprises not so much a basic concern of the Christian faith, but rather something that was missing from the Latin conception of the natural. This is because Greek Christianity knows no superior annex to what is natural. Despite its notable historic import, we will not dedicate ourselves to the opposition of the supernatural and the natural here, regarding it rather as a specific of Latin culture. Instead we will use the words "natural" or "innate," and "nature" in their original Greek sense, which, regardless of religious persuasion, does not allow the use of the prefix "super-," since *physis* used in this sense envelopes even the sacral dimension.

Philosophizing about *physis* is thus an attempt to contemplate the natural, nature, growth, the character of a living being, spontaneity, and the vegetative and generative power of being. It is an attempt at a way of thinking, which touches on everything that comes to be and passes away, everything changeable—that is, on everything that acts out its own living character precisely by its continual flux, and looks for a form that is its own. It is an attempt at thinking about the relations between being and every individual entity that has heretofore emerged or grown up (and hence also its non being). Thus, as expressed by Martin Heidegger, it is an attempt at considering "ontological difference." Such a mode of thinking is, of course, nothing new, and we might ask why, after twenty-six centuries, we can't simply resume with the basic results of the thinker's work? Why can't we straightforwardly refer ourselves to the tradition of "natural philosophy" and continue in it? Why? Because this tradition has enormous discontinuities, and mainly because "natural philosophy" has gained a bad reputation.

In early antiquity, natural philosophy (albeit this term is anachronistic here as it was introduced only at a later date) was, apart from the Eleatic school, almost the only kind of philosophically directed thought. These initial attempts at a particular type of thought were first seriously called into question (leaving aside Parmenides for a moment) by the enlightened generation of early classical Greek sophists. Their thought was aimed at human concerns, towards what was going on in homes and in town squares, at courts and at the assembly. This is not the domain of *physis* but rather the domain of customs, agreements, deals and arguments, of everything the Greeks called *nomo* (dative sg. from *nomos*). Human society is run, and functions, thanks to that which is *nomo*, i.e., thanks to everything that follows from custom, agreement and law, which is thus given. All this can be expressed unambiguously, and so it's also possible to argue about it logically. We can reliably express it and argue about it because, in a sense, it's in our power as immobile. Custom, agreement, and law may well change, but we can talk of them, particularly of agreement and of law, as if they were, for the period of their application, immobile. This possibility arises in the very formulation and origin of an agreement or law. It is an "act of speech" and not a birth or a growth. (Albeit that from a less formal viewpoint even law can share the destiny of everything natural: to be an expression of being, to change itself even with mere interpretation, to pass away.) With the sophists, then, the realm of that which is *nomo* was disclosed as opposite to everything that is *physei*, that is, to everything that comes "from nature," that grows, dies, or changes itself without us having to touch it, and often without us even being able to know about it. The realm of laws and agreements was distinct, and one could therefore consider it precisely, describe it, and pass judgment on it, whereas the realm of nature and the natural appeared as wholly uncertain and of little interest. What the sophists represent, therefore, is a first model for the later division of thought (sciences) into the natural, and the social or humanitarian—the latter of which were placed first at that time because of the benefits of knowledge related to human concerns.

Xenophon's references to Socrates are particularly resonant here. According to Xenophon, Socrates criticized the study of nature, the cosmos, and the gods as being unreliable, and for this reason put the exploration of human questions first. Socrates asks, for example, "whether, just as those who study human nature expect to achieve some result from their studies for the benefit of themselves or of some other selected person, so these students of divine matters expect that, when they have discovered the laws that govern various phenomena, they will produce at will winds and rain and changes of season or any other desired effect [?]" "He himself" explains Xenophon, "always discussed human matters, trying to find out the nature of piety and impiety, honour and dishonour, right and wrong . . ."[1]

Although, unlike the sophists, Socrates' heirs would return to questions of nature and the natural, they did so within the frame of metaphysical philosophy. This philosophy places so much faith in the clarity of truth and the surety of identity, that it sees everything mobile as necessarily lower than the static. In this frame, of course, it is possible to think of *physis* only with difficulty. The loss of understanding for natural philosophy and the complete semiotic transformation of many of its connected expressions can be seen, for example, in Aristotle's term *physiologoi*: "physiologists." This term originally applied to the pre-Socratics in the sense of a "student of nature," but it now means something wholly different. If this were a study of the historical dimension of the philosophy of nature, then we would now turn to an interpretation of Aristotle's *Physics*, and particularly the *Physics* of Chrysippus, that is, to the natural philosophy of the Greek stoics. This shift in meaning was all

---

1   Xenophon, *Conversations of Socrates, Memoirs of Socrates* (London: Penguin, 1990), 71 (1.1.8–16).

the more noticeable in Latinate philosophy because Latin speakers tied on to the Greek sophists in many ways through their pragmatism and formalism, and it was the later Latin speaking Christians that dedicated themselves to "supernatural" concerns. With the single exception, perhaps, of Lucretius Carus, *Physis* is neglected by both Latin pre-Christian and Christian thought.

It was only the syncretism of late antiquity that saw a renewal of natural philosophy in the context of a more general renewal of different kinds of thought. The thinkers close to Hermetism (Poseidonius c. 100 BC) and the writings themselves of the Greek Hermetic corpus testify to this renewal. But with this development, natural philosophy stepped gradually into the sphere of mysterious religiosity, of gnoses and the occult schools, such as alchemy (Zosimus) for example. It became part of an undercurrent, later fed by both Christian and heterodox mysticism. We find it surfacing in the writings of certain Greek ecclesiastical fathers, Latin mystics, and ostensible heretics. Notably, a school of natural philosophy appeared in Chartres in the twelfth century and one at Oxford in the thirteenth. And in this way, it came to see, as part of the Hermetic disciplines of the Renaissance, a new epoch that was interested in everything old and seen from a new perspective, and especially in those things which were obscure.

Among the most philosophical fruits of Renaissance natural philosophy were Ficino's Latin translations of the Hermetic writings. Apart from these, natural philosophy lived also as part of alchemy and astrology. Even the one aspect of Renaissance thought that survived into modernity and defined it—nascent modern science—was often inspired by natural philosophy in many areas of its emergence. On the whole, this inspiration was Pythagorean.

At that time, Pythagorean natural philosophy and Pythagorean science already represented two thousand years of controversy, of opposition to the flow of the rest of philosophy and science. While the rest of natural philosophy was content to be self-contained and not inform the sciences and the polis, Pythagorean thought always aimed directly for philosophy's inherency in biology and politics. So for example, Pythagorean heliocentrism was the result of mystical intuition and the considerations of natural philosophy, not the result of astronomical measurements and calculations. As such, the Alexandrine astronomers would dismiss it from a scientific perspective (Hipparchus), for it did not agree with their observed phenomena. In the late Renaissance, Pythagorean inspiration sought laboriously for its own scientific likeness. Where it did not succeed, it was labeled with the charge of occult obscurantism. (Incidentally, already the archaic Heraclitus protested against the peculiar belligerence of Pythagorean thought.)

Modernity, which began fully only after the formulation of the term "natural law" (by Descartes and his circle) and only after Descartes's separation of soul from bodily things and identification of subject with ego, became badly inclined towards natural philosophy. Natural philosophy represented a dubious relic, hard to classify anywhere, except at best perhaps as charlatanism. After all, even nature was now subject to a "law"! Traditional German philosophy (Schelling), Goethe's spirit-based science, and the philosophically oriented romantic poets in the forefront with Novalis did still attempt a fundamental resuscitation of natural philosophy. But, all of this flowed more readily into theosophy or anthroposophy than into university philosophy, or academic science.

In a newly set-up university lecture course on the philosophy of nature, this sketch of the history of natural philosophy can be distinctly off-putting. It is no accident that in the German speaking sphere, it's often said disdainfully of any pleasing creation of the spirit, that it's some sort of "Naturphilosophie," meaning that it's something unreliable: neither philosophy nor science. It is for this reason also that our title is more cautious. Does this mean then, that we can lean on nothing from the past tradition other than the unquestionable greats such as Anaximander, Anaximenes, Heraclitus, Empedocles and Anaxagoras?

The majority of these ancient thinkers began with natural philosophy in the context of their diverse "investigations" (*historia*), in particular their explorations regarding nature. Can we not then also help ourselves now by using the context of contemporary enquiries made by natural sciences? Can't we utilize the experiences of our current natural sciences? Not so much their results (especially not by generalizing them), but more their heuristics and inner difficulties, their limits and new ideas? Most probably we can, but such a philosophy, showing the relevance of something in science, can only be carried out by someone with a better inside experience of science. In addition, we have, in the 20th century, a hugely expanded philosophy of science in both epistemological and cognitive conceptions, but no-one so far has managed to bring this into a connection with anything experientially natural and simultaneously philosophical; with nature or natural thought.

We will, then, remain on philosophical ground. We can accept help from those philosophers who have shown the deficiency of the modern understanding of nature and the natural in the 20th century: Husserl's phenomenological critique of modern science; Kuhn's structuralist criticism; Heidegger's existential conception of science. And we will regard Patočka's attempt at searching for the "natural world" as the direct precursor of our explorations.

Something has happened to our European humanity. Apart from anything else, we have covered up our own nature and that of others. The natural world now poses an extremely difficult philosophical problem for us. We can clearly see what has happened in the devastated external nature around us. There, it is evident even to those who do not particularly wish to see, or cannot see. We regard it, however, as just one aspect of what we have done to nature, to every form of nature, even for instance to the nature of our own thinking. For our thoughts are equally susceptible, not to mention our feelings. Our main aim is not so much to find a culprit, be it the Latin conception of Christianity, modern science, technology, politics or advertising. Let others solve this ethical problem. Rather, the goal of these enquiries is a philosophical critique of this state, that is, a reasoned understanding and not a judgment—and foremost an attempt at a philosophical contribution towards its repair, not a methodical directive.

What we Europeans (and then everyone else) have committed, was once aptly termed by Zdeněk Neubauer as "the denaturing of *physis*." What this oxymoron suggests is that everything apparently still works for us; denatured matter has only that capacity which we demand of it, and thus work with it is much more secure; but nature and the natural (*natura*) have been sequestered from themselves, from their inner life and spontaneity. Let us hope that the process is not complete and without vestige, at least as regards our thinking. Let's hope that *physis* itself is more powerful than every denaturant.

Novalis championed a similar insight much earlier in a vivid anecdote known to us here through the mediation of Emanuel Rádl, the founder of the Department of Philosophy in the Natural Sciences Faculty at the Charles University:

Allegedly, bodies for the first public autopsies were provided by the hangman, who carefully drowned a chosen convict. The story tells of how, during one such autopsy, an insufficiently carefully drowned convict wakes up and opens his eyes. A wave of panic sweeps across the town square. This horrific scene can be used as an analogy: we dissect not only convicts, but almost everything on earth. We dissect the earth, which we have drowned so carefully that nobody notices it. What terror awaits us then, when the poorly drowned world awakes, what will we read in its face? And what terror awaits, should the world indeed be well drowned?

In order to escape from such strongly romantic gestures, we will, rather than talking of a drowned world, discuss a loss of a sense for *physis*. Doing so is simply more convenient, and no less terrifying. Consider, for instance, that it's possible to make robots even from people relatively easily and serially, through basic education, or ideology or fashion; out of animals and plants it's possible to create the pieces of an agricultural production cycle by a new form of domestication—domestication to the image of the person who has already domesticated himself; and from the rest of the world it's possible to make a storehouse of materials and energy, and a dump. Still, talking about having lost a sense for *physis* not only brings some hope, but it is also in agreement with the ancient image of *physis* as something that grows out of an abyss into which no instrument can reach; from a boundlessness which no tricks can exhaust.

Losing one's sense for *physis* does not necessarily testify to some form of willfulness. A sense for *physis* is somehow lost when we do nothing other than simply follow our quotidian worries and contingent needs for too long, when, in the words of Plato and Patočka, we do not tend to our souls. In the words of Heidegger: when we do not present ourselves to the emerging field of *Dasein* as existences. Sometimes we lose our sense for *physis* ourselves, at least for a little while, out of sensible and respectable reasons such as a fear of the depth of its abyss, of its spontaneity, of its finitude that points us towards death. We fear all of these things. And indeed, it is not wise to play around with these forces. We forget however, that with every fear-driven loss of a sense for the natural our nature is also completely and continually lost. All the more when, running away from the dangers of *physis* we take refuge in the sterile isolation of the safety and comfort of the everyday. Spontaneity that has been thus lost then expresses itself uncontrollably and in spite of calculations. In this way Patočka explains the destructive explosion of nationalism and the wars of the twentieth century. It is only perhaps through such an overlooking and undervaluing of matter that it's possible to explain the rise of modern "materialism," including the enormous enthusiasm surprisingly associated with it.

Thus, in further enquiries we will attempt to rediscover our sense for *physis*. We will draw on our own natural experiences; on the oldest natural philosophy; on phenomenological, structuralist, and poststructuralist analyses of the modern natural sciences within contemporary philosophy.

What we will not do:

We won't form scientific hypotheses, as the Pythagoreans did.

We won't advise the scientists how they should practice science, as certain methodologists do.

We hopefully won't confuse the criticism of science with the damnation of science, as did certain natural philosophers of late modernity.

We won't rely on science in philosophy; only thus can it be philosophical thinking, beneficial to scientists as well.

2. Individual nature. *Physis*. A thing as a grasping of *physis*. The subsoil of phenomena and things. The constitution of things. Things in the world. Things and matter, space, time. Knowledge and reduction. Exemplary entities

Physis is everything that passes through a process of birth and death, coming to be and passing away. Nature includes also its relations, its context. Nature hides itself in its relations to other natures. Across these it relates to the whole, to the connectedness of everything—and it's precisely thereby that nature is natural. It is true on the level of *physis* that "everything depends upon everything else." Although a sentence like this is full of emotive charge expressing a relation to being, it does not convey any information; by itself it means no more that the sentence "nothing does not depend on anything," at least as long as we cannot show "how" and hopefully "in what direction chiefly" this "everything depends on everything" takes place. And so, before we advance to further enquiries, we will attempt to define more precisely the meaning of the word *physis* by referring to one of the thinkers who first brought it under consideration, one who did so straight away in a remarkable fashion: Heraclitus of Ephesus. We will, then, attempt to hold onto this Heraclitus' definition of the word *physis*, despite the fact that what it will signify each time is constantly changing.

Heraclitus' fragment B1 is framed by an exposition of the difference between our human lot of incomprehension and the work of the philosopher. This difference is determined firstly in relation to essential language and secondly in relation to *physis*. It's the second of these approaches that will interest us here.

As uncomprehending beings, our everyday human fate is compared to sleep: ". . . men are oblivious of what they do awake, just as they are forgetful of what they do asleep."[2] This comparison from the end of the fragment completes the idea of who we are, or who the "men [who] ever fail to comprehend" are at the beginning of the fragment. In other places Heraclitus explains this word "uncomprehending" (*axynetoi*) through a playful etymology as those who are "un-communal" or "disconnected" (*a-xynon*) and then also as those "without thought"—in a completely literal translation, those "not-with-mind" (*a-syn-noo*), those who do not take part in thought, in the spirit, in reason (*nus, noos*). Heraclitus' words establish the possibility of consciousness, the possibility of waking up thought, beginning the battle for the communal. Those who "fail to comprehend" do not orient themselves by the earth; they do not experience the power of nature; they are not "present" when nature acts (and for this reason in fragment B34, they are "here" only as "absent," *pareontas apeinai*, only as appearances, even in fact to themselves—B17). The middle section of fragment B1 discusses precisely this gap between the uncomprehending (absentee's) relation to *physis* and the task of consciousness:

> . . . men are like the untried when they try such words and works as I set forth, distinguishing each according to its nature and telling how it is.

The philosopher experiences and also explains both words and deeds. He knows that every experience is already an explanation: an exegesis, an interpretation. One's presence when a word is heard and when an action happens is what establishes direct experience; it forms the basis of an interpretation—that is, one's understanding of the word or action. The experience, the interpretation and the understanding are carried out by distinguishing: "distinguishing each according to its nature." Or even: "distinguishing each of them according to their individual natures." It is thus, and only thus, that a wise person "tells, how it is." Words and deeds manifest themselves through their own power; understanding is the medium in which they show themselves and in which they can also be shown.

Understanding forms relations, thanks to which one can point something out; refer to something through something else, to the connection between one thing and another. An understanding interpretation will

---

2 This, and subsequent translations of Heraclitus' fragments are from Charles H. Kahn's edition, *The Art and Thought of Heraclitus* (Cambridge: Cambridge University Press, 1987).

distinguish what it shows, but distinguish it by forming connections, by associating it with the already acquired contents of consciousness. We cannot comprehend any new word or deed only from the pre-existing contents of our consciousness. This is what makes it new; it's a new encounter with a demand to show and explain; it puts a new task before consciousness. This task is no less than a willingness to change all the existing contents of our consciousness and their usual mutual relations in such a way that the new experience can be had, interpreted, and understood properly, that is "according to nature" and not according to our former preconceptions of it. To have such preconceived opinions, which attempt to subordinate everything to what we already believe we know, is the fate of those who "ever fail to comprehend," of our everydayness, of an insufficiency of presence.

As one of the sayings of the Scholastics goes, *Qui bene distinguit, bene docet* (he who distinguishes well, teaches well). In the context of Heraclitean thinking about *physis*, this is no small demand. Such distinguishing "well" is not always the kind that we have ready at hand, the kind that would offer a consistent explanation or some other formal advantage. Distinguishing well is simply distinguishing by *physis*, according to every individual nature. When this distinguishing does happen to enable an unconflicting explanation, then it's not due to the acumen of our reasoning, which perhaps has skillfully shifted possible conflicts out of the circle of the given theme, but rather thanks to the structure of language and the character of the world. That, of course, is a continual gamble, and one we shouldn't try to facilitate by cunningly overtaking the clarity that we seek. Truth, here, is not the agreement between the statement and the thing, as it is in metaphysical thought. Truth is not yet explicitly under discussion. The original ethos of truth here—disclosure—is the stance experiencing and pointing out each individual nature. This involves the disclosure of something singular, piece by piece, viewing each time the relations it bears to the whole only from one specific place, and not in an overview.

Often we're tempted to aid our understanding in ways other than that recommended by Heraclitus. We're tempted, for example, to seize things firmly, to "fix" them, lock them in a cage or preserve them in order to analyze them thoroughly. Or we're tempted to cut things apart so that we can see what's inside and identify the structure. While doing this we do indeed discern something, but we wrongly regard this as naturally real, by itself. We recognize only that our product has come about through some form of nature. But what we consider to be the inside is nothing more than a new surface, one that nature has presented during the disruption caused to her by our action. The "inner structure" does indeed give evidence about a thing, but differently to the way evidence is given by pointing out the true structure of relations between natures. The use of such aids for knowledge tempts us towards characterizing being (every nature and the connections of natures) similarly to our actions, that is, mechanically, in the manner of a division and a putting together. We could discover much using this technique, but never the actual character of being—we cannot reveal nature. We would distance ourselves from individual natural disclosures, and would attempt instead to compensate for them with the surveyability of general truth. This is exactly the loss of nature already discussed.

In fact, if we wanted to follow Heraclitus' conception of *physis* loyally, then we couldn't even talk of nature as something permanent. We would have to also relativize every heretofore-demonstrated relativity (relatedness) of every local truth in time as well. This is a problem we'll dedicate ourselves to later in a special enquiry into time and synchronicity. But, the question remains: is it possible at all to act out this philosophical ideal of distinguishing according to individual natures? Would that not mean giving up all interference and all of our active standing in the world? Not necessarily, for activity and preservation aren't the same in this respect. To the extent that we shouldn't manipulate, we have to avoid taking part. But we should be active nonetheless; after all, the entirety of this way of thinking is motivated by a call to arms in the battle of life. It is a similar paradox to the one contained in antiquity's original understanding of what constitutes theory, i.e., testimony to the seen. It presumes therefore that we should be good spectators. And a good spectator is precisely the one who is somehow actively uninvolved, who does not follow any interests other than what is to be seen, but actively cares for his own spectatorial position. But in Heraclitus' work, what's at stake is not just the experiencing and pointing out of words, but also of actions. The relation between the uninterfering activity of the philosopher and an action is clearly pointed out already by the oldest occurrence of the word *physis* (incidentally the only one preceding Heraclitus). It is a verse from Homer's *Odyssey*, which (assuming it is not a later addition) is often cited precisely as an illustration of a pre-philosophic conception of nature.

When Odysseus is in danger of being enchanted by Circe, Hermes himself comes to his aid, offering him a magic antidote, which he immediately prepares (*Odyssey* 10.302–3):

So concluding, he tore (lit. uprooted) the healing plant from the ground and showed me its *physis*.

Hermes is the lord of the horizon; he is the one who can cross between the realms of the apparent and the non-apparent. A plant is apparent, but only for those who can identify it. For others it is just a section of green, a piece of field. The wise person is able to distinguish, to differentiate an individual nature. But the god however doesn't pause for the theory. He tears the plant, pulls it out by its roots. With this he definitively detaches it from the background, from the field, and from the earth. And by this he also discloses the root, something wholly hidden before. Even in this action, Hermes respects the boundaries of nature by pulling out the entire root. Yet his "showing of its nature" does not end thereby. The root's nature will show itself in its power, in this case its power of healing, when Odysseus's companions are freed from the enchantment that gave them the appearance of pigs, returning to their innate human nature.

Thus, part of pointing out nature is an ability to distinguish from the background, a capacity for earmarking in the required way, for separating the hidden "roots" of a nature (of a growth) from its foundations, and a capacity for releasing the power of that nature. Similarly, the nature of a bow will only show itself when an arrow is fired, and the nature of a lyre only when it is played. In these cases, artificial things are concerned, but they work because they are full of tension.

Nature is a power that grows out of latency. "Nature loves to hide." It grows into a phenomenon, and as such can be experienced or pointed out, but despite this it is more the growth itself, the principle behind certain phenomena or properties. A wise person can, using an expression of any one nature's power, refer to its essential strength, its character. In the same way he will already have been able to distinguish it through its exterior appearance. That is the general principle of wisdom as expressed by Solon:

Refer to the unapparent through the mediation of the apparent.[3]

The sage experiences, explains and shows individual natures. Hermes showed the nature of the plant chiefly by demonstrating its power to bring Odysseus' companions back to their human nature. However, our

---

3   Demetrius of Phaleron in *Stobaios* 3.1.172.

everyday life, including that of scientific learning, is based on trying to grasp nature as a thing. In order to grip nature firmly and use it for our own ends, we have to detach it entirely from its being, from its "roots"; we have to grasp it as finite and static. It's precisely by doing so that we lose our sense for the natural. One of philosophy's tasks is, then, to disclose even the innate power in a thing, to renew our relationship to the thing as a grasped nature.

A nature is an entity in relation to being. A thing is an entity that we try to understand as it occurs. Our understanding does not usually extend directly to being, but to the roles of things as they occur, to their expressible properties. We can describe a thing using conceptual language. Natures, however, elude solely conceptual description. This is because natures ceaselessly refer to boundlessness in their roots and contexts. A nature has its story (*mythos*), which the sage classifies in the context of language (*logos*). Things can held in speech by finite propositions which are seemingly without context; or with propositions whose context is seemingly specifically and unambiguously determined, for instance by definitions. But there is always more to every real and not merely imagined thing than to each of its finite descriptions. The measure of how much of a thing something is, or how much the thing has been grasped, also determines how detached it has become from the shoreless possibilities and ceaseless changes of nature.

A number of 20th century scholars cite Rilke's verse about a children's game at this point:

Things can be anything,
but you have to tell them first.

Depending on the context, these lines are either a profound statement of natural experience, or nonsense. A wooden spoon in a children's game can be declared a princess, and we can even find the experience for which it is a princess. The counterargument, that it is still only a wooden spoon, attempts to abolish the game or to set up a new one. The game reifies the natural in its own way, distinct from reification on the principle of general utility. It is precisely and only from this general overviewing utilitarian perspective that Rilke's verse appears absurd. But isn't reification on the basis of utility and overview in fact also one of the games? Isn't it just a special kind of game that's particularly hard to step out of? Isn't it a game playing at the global surveyability and calculability of all existence? And isn't this utilitarian reification actually some kind of "meta-game" turned against the unpredictability of local meanings opened up by different playfulnesses; that is, a game aiming to suspend meaning in all other games? And isn't philosophy more the capacity to interpret between individual games, between their local evidences (truths)?

The reification of the natural into a graspable and globally clear shape is such a commonplace for us that we often use phrases like "a non-living thing." Living "things" are, after all, somewhat elusive to us. We feel that life cannot be completely reified without its loss. And we would mind still more if somebody was to understand us as things and dealt with us accordingly. Where does this self-evident feeling come from, suggesting that we should always deal with things in a worse way—a more thing-like way—than the way in which we deal with ourselves? Do we preconceive "non-living things" along the same lines as our artificial creations, or even as mere material for our creations, i.e., as something less valuable? If so, then we are already dealing even with ourselves as things, that is, in relation to some kind of utilitarian aim.

The chief expression of many natures is life. Until it is reified, every nature is, in a sense, alive—although it does not have to be so biologically. It was not by accident that the first ancient theoreticians of the concept of a "thing" (*to pragma*), Empedocles and Aristotle, gave examples of natural things rather than artificial ones. Examples of artificial things have a different role for them—they are examples of human design. When Plato narrates his allegory of the cave (*Republic* 7.514), he depicts something enormously different from the natural world of rich experience outside the cave by pointing towards the shadows of artificial things, he discusses how the gaze of the prisoners is fixed firmly on these shadows thrown across the walls by artificial imitations and artificial instruments, artificially moved. Do we not have here a continuous spectrum ranging from nature, through the natural thing (living and "non-living"), to the artificial thing and finally only its shadow, seen from a fixed and non-free viewpoint? We commit the reifying seizure of nature for mundane and practical reasons. But don't we also do it for the illusion of secure knowledge? Don't we substitute the task of pointing out the natural, that is, the task of local unveiling, with an attempt to see the whole of an entity from a single determined position—an attempt supposed to result in the illusion of an overall truth about being?

Natures are effective because they are full of inner tensions. Reifying a nature means explaining its tensions from one perspective. This works very well with artificial things made deliberately in this way, such as the tension in the bow or the lyre in Heraclitus' examples of the harmonic effect of clashing opposites (B51), or the temperature curve registered in heat engines. Ancient metaphysical philosophy tried to explain every effect and influence in a similar way—through certain basic principles. Aristotle himself explains pre-Socratic thought thus. The reifying grasp is only possible by reducing the wealth of changes and tensions to, for instance, opposed elements. In this way one can come to understand each change as a change of something permanent in itself. This will turn out to be the essential trick of physics. Historically the first description of this sort was Empedocles' "mingling" of elements, which was followed by Democritus' eternal atoms and Aristotle's elements.

We tend to call experiences reified in this manner "objective." Everything that doesn't fit into the reifying description we then consider "subjective." Although these typically modern categories will still demand a separate investigation, it's necessary to begin using them tentatively now because of the very constitution of things in natural experience.

When Aristotle expounds the older thinkers, he asks what they saw the principle of everything (*arche*) as lying in, or in his opinion, what they tried to reduce the wealth of experience to. He asks also what they regarded as the "basis" (*to hypokeimenon*) from which all things grow. Although the word *hypokeimenon* can signify all manner of things, even a bed-sheet, in this context it is the "basis" or rather "base-layer." Aristotle asks what the older thinkers have "underlying" every detail, how they "prop-up" each thing. His answers consist of the elements (water, air, etc.), general things (matter), and the literally "indefinite" (*apeiron*). Cicero comes to translate *hypokeimenon* entirely slavishly and literally as *subiectum*, still retaining all of its contexts and meanings. Of course, *subiectum* will come to be a category in Latin grammar at the same time, meaning the subject of a sentence. And the conception of *subiectum* will continue in this symbiosis of meanings until the end of the medieval period. Descartes, when he says that the *subiectum* is *ego*, still stands in this tradition.

The transformations of modern thought, however, changed the understanding of the subject in such a way that it would probably create unnecessary conceptual confusion if we used the word "subjective" in its original sense, which is, "such that it touches on the basis of everything."

A grasped or imagined thing still continues to be rooted in its subjectivity in that it points towards being. The subjectivity of a thing is a remainder, or an expression of the fact that a thing is a grasped nature. In view of its being held, the thing is already something secure, permanent and finite, but in its relation to the subject, (that is, to its basis, not to human conjectures and caprices) the thing is still open to boundlessness—it relates to being.

Each subject in Latin grammatical and logical terminology also has an object. In this, such formalism pre-empts the subject-object thinking which is fully realized by modern metaphysics. In natural language, an *Obiectum* is an "obstacle"; in its grammatical sense it is an object of a sentence. In Latin philosophical thinking, the object is an obstacle but not in the sense of one inhibiting thought, on the contrary. An object is something that our sight or our thought is stopped by; hence it is something that juts out of an open field of being and draws our attention. After all, I can only lean on things, which, under different circumstances, could be obstacles. A firmly grasped thing is, in itself, already nothing more than a mere "object" and it bears relation to being only in the sentence which has this object in mind, that is, thanks to the subject and thanks to the predicate, which is of course a verb—a word for action or a part of the verb "to be."

Just as we can grasp nature as a thing, so we can understand a thing as an object; and this is another step towards cutting the thing off from its nature, ending with the annihilation of the relationship between nature and being. Grasping things lets us deal with them through our thoughts and with our hands, and to do so in a technical manner, not magically. A technical manipulation differs from a magical one precisely by the objectivity of the item and its defined contexts. The objectification of things allows us to formalize work with objects, so that the work can occur, at least partially, so to speak, on its own: using the formal language of logical calculus, the application of cybernetics, or serial production thanks to formally conceived technology. The truth about an object is separable from the original contexts of the thing, and for this reason it is reproducible, both in the sense that an experiment is reproducible, and in the sense of an exact describability of meaning by unequivocal testimony. The object has no story behind it; it's rid of informal associations, especially the temporal ones.

Science and in particular science's formal disciplines, work with objects. We live our everyday lives among things, although often we regard many of these things in the same way as we do insufficiently precisely fixed objects. We encounter nature in every deeper experience; be it personal, poetic, religious, or philosophical, but we're still tempted to regard it only as a thing. We're most likely to experience the irreducibility of our nature to a thing and that of a thing to an object during an encounter with a living being, particularly another person. Perhaps this is exactly what was meant by the ancient Apollonian prompt *gnothi sauton*, "know yourself," which became one of the maxims of Greek philosophy.[4] It's not a prompt to poke around in one's own "psyche," but rather an appeal to one's own direct personal experience, which is not reducible to a thing and even less so to an object.

We can descend from the everyday level of dealing with things to the level of manipulating objects, whether for a certain type of recognition or for technology. Equally we can go the other way and open our everydayness up to everything natural, being. Perhaps philosophy is precisely the capacity for such transitions, through possibilities such as these, which can't be glimpsed from within themselves. Our investigation can begin with the everyday, the routine, with things.

We all think we know what a "thing" is. We could of course name hundreds of examples—and not just name them, but also point them out in our immediate surroundings. It is, after all, typical for human everydayness to be surrounded by things. However, as usual, the philosophical question problematizes. What is a thing? How is a thing a thing? How does it come about? Why is it that kind of thing? Our apparent knowledge of what things are usually flows only from the fact that we don't, on the whole, ask ourselves these questions about them. Instead, we usually ask ourselves only about certain properties of certain things, or at best, what a given thing is for or about. We do not ask "what is a thing?" But isn't this precisely the constitutive moment of everydayness? Doesn't a thing become a thing precisely because we only begin to question it once it comes down to its properties or some conditions associated with it? In fact, isn't an abnormal glimpse into the power of a thing or the story of a thing an opportunity for us to experience a thing as a grasped nature as it escapes for a moment the reifying power of everydayness? We can experience this even with non-living things, say a pebble from a stream—and even with things that have been artificially produced, since these too can have their own stories, like a house or a teacup perhaps. But as long as we deal with things "pragmatically" we won't be able to open up these stories.

This is yet more noticeable with those "things" that are more like "issues." It's no accident that the Latin word *causa* covers a very wide range of significations. For even what we consider normally to be a bounded physical thing—practically nothing more than an object, can occasionally

---

4   Plutarch, *De E* 17.391f.

show itself to be the matter of a story or a significant issue. Things are issues, and some of them only issues. So for example, *causa* can mean a "case." A case is a kind of set of events somehow describable as a thing; it is graspable. In the legal sense, *causa* requires an issue to be laid out and compared to a model so that all possible stories which touch on that case (witnesses' testimonies for instance) can be reduced by the due method into one clearly and easily described narration, which also makes judgment of guilt and punishment possible. This also is a reification.

The environment of a thing is safe, it surprises rarely and not very radically. It corresponds to our normal speech, expressing and facilitating our everyday needs. It's largely a tool-like language, because it is, primarily, a tool for expression and communication. In itself this tool-like quality of language isn't usually reflected, and isn't usually made use of in any special way. But we can sometimes recall more primal experiences of nature even in this secure, quotidian environment, and simultaneously revivify the language itself. It is thus that poets, for example, look after language's capacity to speak; they're not interested in normality described using language as a tool. Poetic language speaks in other ways, in fact, primarily in ways other than the tool-like. Alternatively, we could set off on a different dangerous outing from the secure environment of things: to complete reification, to objects and the corresponding purely formal language that accounts for them unequivocally. Philosophy, at least in some of its conceptions, attempts both of these abnormal outings simultaneously: reminding us about "primal" nature whilst also trying for an exact formulation of evidence.

Phenomenologists led by E. Husserl analyzed the constitution of things closely from the perspective of the intentions of consciousness, phenomena and the world. Husserl also analyzed the attempt made by modern science to reduce the knowledge of things to the knowledge of objects.[5] On this point we defer to the given literature. The significant result of these investigations for natural philosophy is precisely the ambiguity regarding the constitution of a thing. How we grasp a nature depends on the state of our consciousness. This can be characterized with terms such as: intention, language, discursive mode, horizon of phenomena, the type of the constituted world, even though some of these terms ("discursive mode," for instance) belong more to an index of poststructuralist concepts.

---

5   Edmund Husserl, *The Crisis of European Science and Transcendental Phenomenology*, trans. David Carr (Evanston: Northwestern University Press, 1970).

We construct a thing from phenomena and from the intentions of consciousness, and we construct it in the world, a specific world. A thing without phenomena is unthinkable. And an unthinkable thing is nonsense and not a thing. A thing without contexts in the world is also unthinkable. A thing is always somewhere, and sometime, it has arrived there somehow, and possibly it's for some purpose or at least relates to something. For a thing, the contexts of the world (like subjective viewpoints) represent the primal bottomless depth of nature.

The way a thing is constituted and the type of world in which this thing then occurs, go together. In constituting a thing we already silently presume a certain character of world, certain types of relations into which the thing will fit. The type of world offers a statement about how our consciousness relates itself to being. Only certain types of thing can be in certain types of world. So for example, a little red gnome cannot occur in that type of world where consciousness is biased towards the global assertion of objective perspectives; it can hardly go alongside amino acids. And conversely, in a world determined mainly by religious or poetic experience it's unusual to find electrons or premium bonds, at least they don't have a significant role for orientation in that world.

Here we might ask ourselves the question: how capable are we of actively deciding on a type of world and directing the constitution of things? It would seem that we are not, since we usually regard unsuccessful attempts at unusual constitutions of things, be they common or unusual things, as lies or cheats. Moreover, our relation to being is not a thing, we cannot command it, and we cannot freely manipulate it. Despite this, however, we do experience what seem to be different orders of the world, and this experience is expressed by not only by philosophers and poets, but also by archaeologists. It's as if these various orders of the world, the "worlds" for instance of various ancient or distant cultures represented different styles of reification, as if they corresponded to the different abilities of consciousness. We can also see the notion of the "objective world," which is naïvely derived from modern science as another of these cases. Although we cannot manipulate freely our relation to being or therefore to the world itself, being is always fuller than our relation to it; the possibilities of consciousness always greater than we can at that moment realize, and nature always richer than each of its reifications. It was on this understanding that magic was based in old types of world. After science had attempted to disclose the world as unambiguous we saw again the polysemy of experience and language and the plurality of the world. The poet and linguist, Emanuel Frynta says of one literary genre that "it is an artistic expression of an entirely definite experience with the world. It is a manifestation, or rather let us say, an analogy for the recognition which has come fully to the last several generations: that reality does not have one transparent and easily discoverable plan, that it is multi-layered, polydimensional."[6] Attempts at a philosophical evaluation of this experience have been made, as for example in the work of Zdeněk Neubauer. A similar experience also has political associations in the theories and practices of a pluralist society. An experience of this sort forms the bedrock of postmodern thought.

The philosophy of nature doesn't want to devalue science. In fact, it doesn't even want to devalue the results of an objectivist conception of science. Rather it only tries to classify science, including its specific, typically modern conception, into the context of the pluralistic character of experience. It wants to classify scientific statements into the significatory contexts of different modes of speech. For a scientific approach to experience, it is typical to incorporate far more extensive and exact reductions than the usual everyday reductions of natures into things. So for instance we might say in everyday life that something is green. The scientific explanation makes this more precise by translating it into a different language and a different type of world: its greatest reflectivity is around the wavelength of 0.52 microns. Behind each of these stands the natural experience of something green—an experience one can explain as being an experience of the power of some nature, that nature for which greenness is an expression of its power. We'll need to dedicate a further enquiry into the problems of reductive knowledge. For the moment however, let us just remember that every reduction, the everyday and the objective scientific one, affects not only what it simply reduces, that is, the nature of a thing or an object, but also the whole world.

Each thing is always a thing in the world. We can talk about that thing and that world with the many terms used to describe their properties. Among these, a special place is held by concepts that cannot be left out in types of world accessible to us: matter, space, time. Although we can reasonably deal with something immaterial (e.g. a perfect triangle as a geometrical shape, or a number or logical operator), something is clearly missing from the corresponding formal "worlds" of geometry, arithmetic, and logic. They are missing temporal relation. Their precision and fascination is paid for by the obscurity of their essence. Mass

---

6   Emanuel Frynta, *Zastřená tvář poezie* [*The Veiled Face of Poetry*] (Prague: Nakl. F. Kafky, 1993), 110.

is a special category that gives evidence about our world, however it informs differently in the environment of the everyday world of things than in the environment of precise science. One's conception of mass determines the conception of the world and hence also of all the thinkable things in it. Similarly with space, and even more so with time, the most enigmatic of philosophical themes. The horizons of matter, space and time are entirely fundamental to the constitution of a thing.

Often our thinking is determined involuntarily by what we imagine an example of an entity to be. Examples prefigure for instance, our reducing grasp, that is, what and to what we want to reduce. We're trying, after all, to prop-up our knowledge with something that *is* in some more fundamental or more "actual" way. An involuntarily-thought example of a model entity directs attention to certain domains of phenomena. Certainly, there's a difference between taking a metabolizing life form as one's paradigm and a perfectly rigid body, or something on the molecular chemical level. Similarly, we'll be led to different conclusions when we consider in turn the defining human ability as reason, intuition or feeling. Every culture, epoch, and area of science has its own prevalent paradigms and its own favored typical properties. I.e., it has its own examples of what "is" in a regular way and how it manifests itself. These examples are the preferred types of reduction, by the help of which people of a given area orient themselves through experience. Sometimes paradigms are loudly declared, whilst at others they are tabooed, particularly in areas of sexuality or finance. A change in a paradigm testifies to a change in the conception of the world. Often we do not understand a testimony simply because, despite the fact that it seems quite general, it presumes certain unspoken and cointended exempla, which of course we are not party to at that moment.

What should the paradigm of the philosophy of nature be? Philosophy cannot proceed in this way if it wants to remain faithful to its investigation of being *qua* being. The example of essence is essence alone, every essence. And for the philosophy of nature? The natural, *physis*? The natural is effective and it *is* in this sense, but it only becomes an objective entity after some certain grasping. For the natural is the relation between an entity and the depths of being. Nevertheless, every natural experience can be an example of something more fundamental than all grasping interpretations. And a special example of *physis* can be our personal nature, that is, the natural experience of one's own being and the requirement to know one's self: *gnothi sauton*, the possibility of orientation within one's possibilities.

3. The cosmos. The world as the background of phenomena and the context of things. The world as the unity of horizons. Parts and wholes. The world and the paradigm of phenomena and the grasping of nature as a thing. The world and language. The plurality of the world

A lost sense for *physis* becomes evident in damage caused to the world. Its consequences are easily seen in defiled outer nature and in the devastation of the countryside. But it's more difficult for us to see the corruption of our relation to being and the devastation of our own thought. What else does the act of "damaging the world" carry with it? What is a world? How can it be damaged, and how can it be cleaned?

We routinely use the word "world" in various senses, usually we mean by it some kind of whole, everything. Sometimes we mean only our planet, which is, of course, a sufficiently large whole for most of our daily needs. However, should concerns fall to us that are not so mundane: astronomical or religious concerns for example, then our planet shrinks to a mere fragment of an incomparably larger and richer whole. At other times a broader area alone is enough for us to start talking about "the wider world." Simply put, the world must always be sufficiently big for everything that is going on or is being thought about to still be well within its "circumference." At other times again we use the word "world" to signify existence "he came into the world." The world for us is the space of existence, of reality. These days we use the Greek word for the world, *kosmos*, predominantly as a borrowing in astronomical and philosophical contexts. But what did this Greek word originally signify, and how did its meaning assert itself in early philosophy?

In the oldest Greek, pre-philosophical usage, *kosmos* always signified something to do with order, be it an order's utility or its beauty. The Ionian philosophers shifted these meanings to an order of nature and society. And the word *kosmos* thus came to mean both a natural order and a social order reflecting the natural order. In the original Ionian pre-philosophical conception, this order is not imprinted on nature from without, but is its own order; it is the coexistence of opposites in the frame of a common whole. The supreme expression of this natural order is not just the regular movement of the heavens, but also the tendency towards the equalization and reformation of differences such as hot-cold or male-female. The mythical representation of the ordering of the cosmos is Orpheus's music, to which all animals listen, the wild and the tame alike, and without which they would devour each other. It is an allegory for opposites inside the frame of the cosmos: if wolves and panthers were placed in the same isolated enclosure as lambs and rabbits, grass and cabbages, they would come to an early demise, dying of hunger; whereas, in the world, predators also hunt prey but the equilibrium is maintained, the world runs on and does not exhaust itself. Here we see the probable inspiration for Euripides's famous utterance, "unaging cosmos of immortal nature" (fr. 910), evidently a paraphrasing of Anaxagoras. In such a conception the center of the cosmos is the sky, as it was already on Achilles' famous shield (*Iliad* 18.483). There's no place for anything super-cosmic here; there's not even a reason for it, just as there's nothing "super-natural." The celestial beings are still the backbone of the world, but this world is perceived as an order of *physis* with aspects of beauty and justice that don't exclude harsh and cruel acts—since it is by playing out these acts that the equilibrium of the world's course is enacted.

For the first philosophers the world was also "that which is shared" (Heraclitus' *to xynon*), into which we step when we wake up. In this sense the world is then "one" (B89):

> The world of the waking is one and shared, but the sleeping turn aside each into his private world.

Unwoken people perceive only the order of their own property, say their own house—or the order of that which they have an ordered knowledge of, as for instance numbers. They see the individual orderings of a few things. However, he who wakes up into a connection with the world's being will glimpse nature's order. One shared world does not appear to him through a reduction of everything to one principle, or even by some kind of generalization of all particulars, but rather through experiencing the unity of antagonisms within *physis*. The liberal order (*kosmos*) which opens itself up in this way, is not translatable into any one unequivocal globally-glimpsable ordering (B124):

The fairest order in the world is a heap of random sweepings.

The *cosmos* is not the opposite of individual natures being independent. Rather, it is their mutual relationship, a medium of relations and differences. It is the opposite of individual partial orderings compelled into being by an exterior force and for some purpose. From this perspective, the modern idea about there being one objective world is more of a rational extrapolation of the local orderings of sleepers rather than a disclosure of the *kosmos*. In the Ionian philosophical disclosure, the *kosmos* is a natural order; it is not made, as everything in the domain of *physis* is not made (B30):

The ordering, the same for all, no god or man made . . .

This is not an atheist expression contesting the divine role. Rather, it expresses an experience of *physis*, which of course is not made, either by people or gods. Christians will call this view of the world *creatura*, Creation, not production. The world is neither a product nor a project.

In our everyday normality we don't experience the world directly; we silently presume it. Things captivate us, but each of those things is, upon looking more deeply, a thing in the world. For us, disclosing the world lies in the extraordinary: in the harmony of nature; in the beauty of the sky, stones or flowing water; in the rhythm of life. The philosophical investigations of the phenomenologists can refer to the world thus, as the context and horizon of each thing.

I see a flower in the garden. I can grasp it as a thing, and if I choose I can also manipulate it as a thing. I can comprehend it in its objectified state as a part of the inventory of the garden, or as an opportunity for attaining something—whether it be money or "aesthetic value." The flower could also, however, inspire a poetic discovery of nature or become an opportunity for experiencing nature's rhythms. And it could also be an opportunity for a philosophical disclosure of the references a thing makes to the world. We could ask after the properties of the flower and name various phenomena: shape; color; smell. To be able to enquire in this way, however, the flower must already be here, and we must be able to see it. The flower is here precisely because it has filled itself with shape, color, and smell; it's through these, its phenomena, that we perceive and distinguish it. We don't even have to be able to name it. The simple fact that we have noticed it and can talk about it means that we have differentiated it from its background—that we have related certain perceived phenomena with something definite, with this flower. The abilities of our senses and our thought alone are insufficient for this. The flower itself had to offer the opportunity by growing here. It distinguished itself from its bed of earth and from the surrounding plants first, and for this reason we can distinguish it as well.

We could imagine the same flower elsewhere. We could imagine a different flower in its place. Both are thinkable. The flower would always, however, be somewhere. This "somewhere" is a reference to the world. It does not, in the least, have to mean that the world is merely a big repository for things, extendedness itself. This "somewhere" is foremost an attribute of existence and connectedness. Every "somewhere" has its "next-to" and this applies equally in the sense of connectedness, as it does in the sense of similarity. I could imagine, for instance, a different but similar flower in the same place, one "related" in some way. I could also imagine a different flower of the same species. It is one thing to distinguish a species and another to be able to distinguish this particular flower. This flower, however, cannot be any differently than as this particular one, and as a flower of a particular type. Here we touch upon the awkward question of species determination, the justness of which we still have to investigate. For now though, it's enough for us to know that our thought tends towards classifying things in categories of species, and that natures give a sufficiency of pretexts for this tendency.

We don't need to know, for instance, the history of the flower. We don't have to know whether it grew here "itself" as a weed, or whether somebody planted it, and if so, who, under what circumstances and why. Even not knowing this history it's unthinkable for there not to be one. Nothing in the world is ever otherwise than somewhere and at some time, under some circumstances; nothing can be without its story. We're simply able to detach and reinterpret this story in the associations of our own human narrative. We can also grasp a thing reifiedly, even as an object, i.e., ahistorically. We are capable of reducing the course of events. This is precisely the reifying grasping of nature and the consequent objectification of a thing already mentioned. But in fact, even an objectified thing still carries with it traces of its nature, of its origin and situatedness. Metaphorically speaking, "it has a navel," a sign of its having been born, similar to the signs of its progress and its transience. These days an amusing analogy to this problem is the medieval debate over whether Adam should be depicted with a navel or without one. In support of the bellybutton was the fact that he had been created and not produced; against it was the fact that in the frame of the Genesis myth he was not born of a woman, and for this reason he should bear the memory of his origin in a different form. Each thing always has a "navel" or something analogous, something that refers back not only to an embryonic state in the sense of a generational origin, but also to how the thing was detached from the background of everything and the contexts of the world, always expressing a kind of constitutional difference in respect to its bedrock or surroundings.

A flower can also occasionally surprise us with some of its properties. Of course, we regard certain types of surprise as impossible in this world. We presume, for instance, that flowers have a reverse side—the side we cannot see at exactly that moment. We presume that we could see the other side from a different angle and that between these two viewing angles there is a smooth transition. This apparently self-evident fact, the denial of which would be absurd, is one of the fundamental pieces of evidence about the world. Rear sides of things sometimes don't surprise, and sometimes they do, but they will never surprise us through their non-existence or absolute disjointedness. A similar piece of evidence about the world is also the experience that a living nature will soon die if it is isolated from outside connections, from its surroundings, the world. Likewise with the experience that although everything living and non-living can be separated into pieces, the reverse process is more difficult—and living things often don't survive it. The relations of things to the world always allow us to presume something in advance about even entirely unknown things, as for example the reverse side. Simultaneously however, they complicate all of our attempts for exact and unambiguous statements.

The basic relations of things to the world, which we have seen with the flower, also apply to non-living things, even to artificial things. A teacup, for instance, has not grown up or fulfilled the shape of its species determination in the biological sense. But it's nevertheless absurd to imagine a teacup without a maker, or one with no relation to our notions of the shape, properties and function of a teacup. And teacups also always have a rear side, even should some practical joker try to make one that went beyond all our usual expectations in every possible way. Neither can a teacup be otherwise than somewhere and somehow with its own history. Likewise we can divide a teacup into pieces, during the study of the properties of materials for instance, but from those pieces we'll only succeed in putting back together a more-or-less effective imitation of the original teacup; it won't be the same.

Every phenomenon manifests itself against some background; it is a contrast as well as a connection; it shows itself thanks to the difference in the tensions of natures, and linguistic differences make speech about it possible. Every section of the background—the context of the phenomenon—is in the same position in regard to some wider background, even though this "wider" does not always have to be wider only in the spatial sense. The world is not the totality of things, for already the number of things, even if it was to be infinite, depends on the perspective of their reification and objectification. The world is not the sum of everything, but rather a contextuality. The world is more in things having their surroundings and associations. The world is mutuality. The world is holistic, but not in the sense that we could imagine a maximum whole, rather in the sense that every individual entity somehow refers to the whole as to a perspective of mutual relations.

The very concept of the whole contains paradox. It's true that in routine situations dealing with things we are able to distinguish the parts and the wholes, and for this reason we think the whole to be the sum of its parts, or at least, that the whole is always greater than a part. Historically these self-evidences belong to the basic armory of Aristotelean thought and Euclidean geometry, but they only become self-evident through a certain method of reification and rationalization; their absolute validity is a decision in favor of a definite type of understanding and perceiving. Nature differs from things precisely in that it's not always already decided what is a part, whence, how, and in what sense it's a part, or even how such hypothetical parts stand relative to each other, and whether or not they're also parts of something else. The obscurity of the whole and its parts, as long as all are in fact only "its" and only parts, are now in need of closer examination. In particular we need to consider whether the "whole" is a whole at all.

Sometimes we encounter types of parts that clearly advertise themselves as parts, even when we hold them complete in our hands. Take, for example, the shard of a teacup on the floor. Clearly we can see that if we had all of the pieces then we could theoretically put the cup back together. The question is simply whether this is practically possible and whether afterwards the cup would be just as good. Thanks to our experiences of complete teacups we recognize a shard as obviously a part; indeed, this is often accompanied with a sense of regret over fragmentariness, or at other times perhaps by a sense of the intellectual joy an archaeologist receives at being able to identify what sort of a teacup it was. A more alarming effect would be created in an encounter with a torn-off hand by the roadside. That would manifest its incompleteness more drastically, and remind us of our own fragmentability more personally than the shard of teacup. Conversely, a leaf fallen from a tree onto a path in the park wakens nostalgia in us, but points more towards the regular fall of nature's cycle. Not scientific knowledge alone, but all of our everyday concerns and technology rely on fragmentation, on biting off, cutting apart, mincing, and laying out, often so we can then do something more, changing the relations between parts and wholes. A cement factory will first grind up broken stone, then fire it into cement powder that is then mixed into cement, and which should finally then harden somewhere as a new whole. We cut off, cut up, cook and eat . . . Metabolism (probably including the metabolism of thought) is the secret of parts and the whole. Wholes in this instance could be a human or a goat. This is not only because we can clearly distinguish a human from a goat, but also because we can discern various individuals of each species. But how would it be with grass? What would a single entity be, a whole? Such questions make little sense with most plants, and the sensible botanist tends to concern himself with the number of species or the total biomass in one given area. After all, sweet flag overgrowing a pond is often only one organism, one plant. And what about mushrooms with their hidden, fibrillar, and unbelievably tangled root-systems? And what about our thoughts, sometimes proudly autonomic like a goat on a cliff, at others yet more stealthily entwined into the unknown than the root systems of mushrooms among the roots of forest trees? Perhaps we can hold complete in our hands only the shards of some reification, at least where *physis* is concerned.

Usually we are capable of recognizing parts as parts—all that is needed is a little circumspection lest we mistake one for a whole. We can compare parts to each other, both by their size and their position in the whole, and also by their mutual relations and roles in the whole. When we point out a part, what we are pointing at and what we are talking about is obvious. This is not so with a whole. Imagine I draw an oval on a blackboard, point to it and say "a part." I draw another and say "a different part." For illustration I put them both together in one border and everyone can see that they are two separate parts, or what could be formally labeled two subsets, straightforwardly spatially and, moreover, only two-dimensionally distributed. We are tempted to point at the common enclosure and say, "a whole!" Except that this boundary is only a whole for the two parts (albeit possibly also one for many other parts which are as yet unknown, perhaps even from different viewpoints). It's surely not one for any third oval outside it. It is definitely possible to be a "whole" for certain determined parts. This makes sense. But is such a whole truly a whole? As a concept, the whole is inherently paradoxical unless we add that we're thinking of a whole only for such and such, but then it's no longer so entirely holistic a whole because from other perspectives it's partial. In fact, I can often show it to be a part of some greater whole, that is, part of another larger part of something else. This is not just a question of spatial size, but also other possible types of relations. Even when I satisfy myself by representing ever-richer types of relations with a mere 2D distribution on the blackboard, then in time I will come across the boundaries of the board. In this illustration it represents the world, and its edges represent the horizon of a given view of the world. But the world is not limited by a certain size. I could imagine a bigger blackboard, I could add more dimensions, but where would an actual whole lie? The universe? Every part has its neighborhood, and many a part is a whole for its own parts.

A genuine whole, the universe or the world, however one pleases, is always such a neighborhood for every part, overstepping every determined horizon of phenomena and thought. The ancient thinkers called this "the encompassing, the embracing"[7] and considered it something divine.

The background (context) is the horizon of phenomena. The neighborhood of each thing is the horizon of that thing—and this does not only concern spatial neighborhoods, but also the webs of relations that are comparatively independent of spatial or even temporal localization. Every thing is perceivable and thinkable only in regard to some background and before some horizon. This is inherent in the basic structure of the world. I do not notice the horizon when I investigate a thing, and I investigate at most a few of its relations to its neighborhood. Despite this however, I can, whenever I choose, think about or look at something in that neighborhood or in the direction of the horizon. Although the horizon is somehow glimpsable, it is not a thing in itself. It is simply an aspect of things in the world seen or thought about from a definite perspective. When the perspective is changed, then the horizon of the thing changes too. The same thing, in different associations can sometimes manifest itself differently. The countryside, when we walk through it on

---

7   *to periechon*, *periechein*, see for example Anaximenes B2.

an outing, also has its horizon. More precisely, it's with respect to some horizon that we notice everything that we can see or think about in that landscape from one perspective. By walking, or by changing one's way of thinking, this horizon changes. Sometimes this is almost smooth, the new horizons being very similar to the last ones, but some as-yet unconsidered horizons can be surprisingly different. In the frame of these we glimpse unexpected things or unexpected associations of things known from elsewhere. This is another of the fundamental pieces of evidence about the world.

We can talk of the world as a kind of "horizon of horizons," as a context of contexts, connection of connections. Yet this is probably not a very precise designation. It's already not so because it tempts us to help ourselves with a further iteration (of the type: the horizon of the horizon of the horizons, which is almost surely nonsense). Probably it would be more exact to talk of the world as a mutuality of horizons, which despite their variety and sometimes surprising differences, do in fact share something that establishes the togetherness of the world. It is not the common denominator of things or even their horizons, but rather some kind of unity of all these relations.

The world is capable of surprising us. Despite this, we can, reasonably justifiably, make certain assumptions about it. To be precise, we can probably take for granted whatever relates to the reciprocal connection of all things. So for instance, there is a group of things and events that we fairly correctly regard as impossible, even though we know nothing about them. Many of these would simply disturb the course of the world so much that it would no longer be a world. Many strange and wonderful things happen in the world, but not "miracles" (the inverted commas signify that the standard understanding of miracles is excluded, not the miracles themselves—for the world is itself a medium for miracles, *physis*). We don't believe the thief who claims that the money jumped into his pocket on its own, whether because of its coming to life and aiming for home or as the result of an unlikely, but not entirely impossible agreement of directions according to the Brownian motion of its particles. A table in a refectory doesn't usually rise up into the air, and I don't usually have to watch out lest I fall upwards into the sky. Baron Munchhausen would not fit into our world. In our world water flows from top to bottom, and we are more likely to see a cat chasing a mouse than a mouse chasing a cat. The conception of a "natural law" developed in early modernity is based on precisely this natural dispensation. The stoics captured this measure of natural "lawfulness" already in their term "the habit of nature," but the modern concept of "natural law" adds to this a certain precise formal objectification of a particular described course of events. Thanks to primary school and the role of technology, our experience of the world in many respects is formed not just by the way things usually unfold, but also, in fact, by an explanation of certain "natural laws." Because of this, our experience of the world doesn't agree well with diverse variations of possible thinkable and imaginable styles of world. Often these are summarily ranked alongside the parodic world of Baron Munchhausen stories.

Our everyday world is colored by the attempt for a global overview of truth in "objectivity." It is damaged by many of the consequences of the techno-scientific approach to reality. This however is not the only damaging, and perhaps not even the fundamental damaging of the world. Our everyday world has always been the frame of some reification. As such, it's the frame only for certain connections. Grasping reification always reduces nature—and a reduced similarity of mutual relations referring to the world corresponds to this. Our world's incompleteness is proportionate to the extent to which a grasped thing can never represent a whole nature in the depths of its fullness.

Our world is also artificial in many of its traits. This is because we often grasp a thing through a certain assumption about its relations, by predefined, even perhaps merely-suggested hypotheses about the world. A thing that is thus inauthentically grasped, instead of revealing its relations to being, points out the projections of our preceding hypotheses about the world. Often during the reification of a thing we not only overly detach it from the context of the world, but, what is more, we insert it into unsuitable contexts. We form purposeful relations, sometimes for so-called advantage, at other times out of pure willfulness or ignorance. The world then reveals itself to us as an artefact of our grasping of things; and the style of this world, that is, the manner of relations in it and the layout of its possibilities, becomes more of an expression of our method of grasping. This world corresponds to the paradigmatic state of our consciousness. A paradigm—our model of essence and knowability—then determines not only the method of grasping things and the character of the world, but also the type and scope of phenomena which our experience can encounter.

The partial quality and artificiality of our world will stand out particularly in a confrontation with other "worlds," with other partial ones as well as perhaps ones with partially artificial routines of phenomena and grasping. What is concerned now is not Baron Munchhausen, whose stories illustrate the unfathomable quality of the world as a frame for any story rather than a genuinely differently experienced world. Any sufficiently distanced culture can be an example of alternative structures of experiential horizons, whether in terms of time, space, religion, race or language. We talk quite justifiably about the "world of ancient Egypt." Things are grasped in it from a slightly different side, so that sometimes different things appear as important and others don't appear at all. The structure of the mutual links of phenomena is different, and different also are the means towards orientation in that world and the means to knowing things in it. Even the world of archaic Greek culture, which is fairly close to us, has a surprisingly different structure than the classical world, let alone the modern one. A careful reading of ancient poetic texts reveals people who differ only negligibly from us, but who are situated in differently constructed associations of the world. The beauty of knowing another culture comes not merely from knowing unusual things, but in disclosing unusual types of relations between things and phenomena. Perhaps it could be said: "The number of types of world that you perceive, think, and deal in, is the number of times you are a human."[8]

What about the "reality" of these many worlds? Is ours the genuine one, or at least the closest to being genuine? Or are they all real in some way? Is there such a thing as a "genuine" or "real" world? What could these terms, designated for statements about things and the knowledge of things, possibly mean in regard to the world? Every world is the self-evident structure of the relations phenomena have to their backgrounds, the structure of differences, of the relations of things to the connections and horizons of perception and grasping. Another aspect of the world is the method of mutual connections between horizons. And during all of this, a role is played by every individual nature, by our *physis*, by the structure of consciousness showing how the subconscious surfaces, and by language, which we not only communicate in, but also in which alone we think and perceive.

Language and the world mutually correspond. Language shows connections. A word in a language and a thing in the world mirror each other, but do so slightly differently in each situation or each language: in a different web of differences. The world is the horizon for a thing, and language the horizon for a word. We can grasp a nature as a thing from various viewpoints, just as a word can, in various contexts, change

---

8   A variation on the slavic proverb: "the number of languages you know is the number of times you are human" [translator's note].

its comprehendible meanings and thereby also change the significatory relations of its surroundings—certain sentences for instance. Every language (say Czech or Greek) becomes aligned to its culture's type of world through its long-term evolution. The culture expresses itself with a language, and that language is one of its perspectives for grasping nature and noticing phenomena. The spectrum of words is aligned with the usual reification of natures. Grammar and sentence construction are aligned with the types of relations between things that a given culture experiences most sharply. It's possible within every language to create special substructures for unusual purposes. In extreme cases such substructures could be artificial, purely extensional languages, as, say, the language of formal logic or a programming "language." Each such substructure enriches language with new possibilities, but in itself is always poorer than the original language and speech as a whole. Each such substructure gives evidence of a certain "slice" of culture provided by the world, one that enhances an experience of the world, but is in itself inferior and for the most part artificial.

Among the illusions of modern European culture are also illusions regarding some one basic world language, that is, illusions about the unity of the world in the sense of its global overviewability and expressibility. We do not mean by this illusion of a "universal language" any of the world languages, even less so Esperanto. That is the realm of the communicative role of language, where forming a character of the world is secondary. The universal language, which medieval scholastics were already on the lookout for, should theoretically be logic or mathematics. But can any substructure of "natural" languages give evidence about anything other than again the substructure of their cultural world? Isn't such a disclosure of "one single world"—that is, the disclosure of a privileged world or "universe"—in fact merely a disclosure of one slice through our everyday world? We'll need to investigate this further, for precisely such effectively-run slices through our world are essential for our overall experience of it. Let us return, however, to the question of whether there really are more worlds, or just one that is genuine. The word "genuine" has shown itself to be misleading, for it insinuates that the world is something in the manner of a thing, something that we can look at. It's therefore better to ask: Is an experience of nature classifiable into many mutually various webs of references or is one web of relations underlying? The determination of nature in itself calls for the first option. Only from various reifying perspectives can a certain nexus of relations or type of horizon appear as "underlying," that is, when it underlies a certain possibility of reification. However, these diverse worlds, diverse styles of natural horizons are not entirely discrete from each other. This is firstly because of the fact that they are worlds; secondly, because there is, after all, something mutually similar between them; and mainly because it is possible to interpret between them, just as it is possible to interpret between the languages of different cultures—although it is a much more basic type of feat than a linguistic one.

Each "world" has its "worldwideness": the structure of the horizons of phenomena. We could therefore talk about the plurality of worlds. But likewise, we could also reserve the word "world" for the "worldwideness" of these various worlds of relations. In a related way, we could use "world" for the possibility of interpreting, of crossing between diverse ways of orientation in experience, between diverse standpoints for the grasping reification of natures. This decision appears to agree well with the bulk of the oldest philosophical tradition, in particular with Heraclitus' use of the term *kosmos*, that is, with the style of thinking we drew on for the conception of *physis* or nature. Thus one can understand occasional statements about the plurality of worlds (even in antiquity there are statements in which *kosmoi* occur in the plural) not as statements about multiple "universes" as objects, but as a correction for the narrowed signification of the term *kosmos*. They correct the state where "one" in the order of the world is construed hierarchically, when the order of the movement of the world is reduced to a determined order. In such situations, talk about the plurality of worlds points towards the wealth of the horizons of experience and their relations, to their reciprocal irreducibility, and to the impossibility of explaining the world in one language absolutely and without remainder.

In this way the world presents itself to us as a basis for the possibility of interpreting between. It does so as the foundation for the possibility of comprehending nature, and as the opportunity for comprehending many foreign expressions of a different grasping of nature. This world isn't something that we can point out, neither is it self-evident. It must be continually opened up in the battle for experiencing and understanding. Knowledge of the world is not translatable into a revelation of some kind of objective order then, but happens in every individual act of experiencing, comprehending and especially interpreting between. Truth is not the disclosure of the whole in the sense of a complete disclosure of all things. It always reveals some new circle of connections: the relations or effects of nature, the meanings of a word. Truth isn't the shared property of common sense and it doesn't reside in the subject-object proposition. It resides in phenomena, in effecting and in interpreting between. Truth is in every such opening-up of something to a whole that respects the plurality of being, the polysemy of every individual nature. In the depths of each nature hides the basis of truth—the foundation for pluralities of meanings, insights and statements.

4. The natural world. Surroundings, the everyday world, the world-view. Reduction in objectivist science and phenomenological reduction. The natural world as a problem of life

Our enquiry so far has indicated all that the world could mean. Our world is damaged, and we can legitimately blame certain aspects of this damage on technology. But isn't technology merely a medium by which we can realize, in a palpable and panoptic way, the more fundamental damaging of the world that we're responsible for? Isn't the world always already somehow damaged, just as humans are, simply because people have detached themselves from it—because a human being is a peculiar nature that has come to see itself also as standing in some respects apart from the rest of nature? Most old myths answer this question affirmatively. They tell either about the fall of man (Jewish myths for example), or of how the world became ordinary and old (most myths); about how humans and the world need to be cleansed, or even as the Christian conception has it, redeemed. Are we therefore to return to the original world by being cleansed? Since we've already experienced much else apart from myth, say philosophy or science, however, we immediately go on to ask: which, or at least, of what sort is, or was this "original world"? Although we're happy to look back nostalgically at Paradise or the Golden Age, we're not seriously going to strive after a simple return to "natural humanity," the unseparatedness of consciousness from nature. The slogan "back to the trees" presents neither an attractive option, nor a practically achievable one.

The contemporary period is notably enriched by the many discoveries of ancient wisdom, thanks to which we are ceasing to be isolated from the archaic style of perception. But although modern technological sciences may no longer be the only frame for our perception and understanding, we still have to face up to the temptation for a mere escape to archaic forms. A return to an all-encompassing unseparatedness would be nothing more than compensation for the modern fragmentation of our world. Is it possible, despite this, to philosophically explore the "natural world," a world of natural experience not formed by the technological sciences or any other of our manipulative designs? Can philosophy unveil the natural world now, after the all-encompassing power of myth has fallen apart, indeed even after scientific objectivity has colored our experience of the world and provided us with unforeseen rational and technical means for its devastation?[9] Can philosophy discuss the world in this way at all? Can the ancient parallels between the structure of the cosmos and the structure of the *polis*, and between the experience of the world and the experience of society, offer us anything at this "advanced stage"?[10] Can the natural order in the cosmos and in human beings be straightforwardly cleansed of the crust of our devastations of both exterior nature and the morality of our lifestyle?[11]

Jan Patočka showed the way to the natural world through subjectivity, leading to the fundamental holistic experiences of human beings (relationships with one another, work, engagement). Subjectivity always enables a descent to naïve experiences. The philosophy of nature would like to understand this revealed "natural world" as a "world of natures." But isn't such an exposition of the natural world merely an expression of naïve objectivism, from which someone could presume that under all the reifying grasping there lies some form of "reality itself," some form of "naked truth"? This objection would surely be valid if we confused nature for an object. For we can't imagine that beneath each of our objectifications of experience there's some "natural object," of which we can partially take hold each time. This is not in the character of *physis*. Every *physis* grows from the subsoil (*hypokeimenon*) or rather from boundlessness (*apeiron*) and has therefore also a degree of indeterminacy. The "world of natures" should not be a world of any "genuine and original" things, but rather a structure of the relations to boundlessness as mediated by phenomena and differences (opposites) in their foundations.

---

9   See Jan Patočka, *Přirozený svět jako filosofický problém* [*The Natural World as a Philosophical Problem*] (Prague: Čs. spisovatel,1992).

10 See Václav Bělohradský, *Přirozený svět jako politický problém* [*The Natural World as a Political Problem*] (Prague: Čs. spisovatel, 1991).

11 See Erazim Kohák, *The Embers and the Stars: A Philosophical Inquiry into the Moral Sense of Nature* (Chicago: University of Chicago Press, 1984).

Let's return, however, from attractive hypotheses to the safer ground of investigating the structures that accompany our relationship with the world. Our everyday lives play themselves out in some kind of setting. We live in a certain landscape, which has its characteristic features, certain relations amongst its horizons. Likewise we live in a certain echelon of society. In daily life, we scarcely notice the structures of horizons; they present themselves to us more in a lifelong feeling for a usual order. In everyday perception we don't concentrate on the structure of horizons, but rather on typical things and events. The world which surrounds us is characterized by one river or stream and a few hills; the countryside by dust or mud and the few types of animals and plants that we notice; society by a few friends and enemies, colleagues or neighbors. Our everydayness sees great significance in artificial things and the manufactured: kitchen utensils; furniture; clothing; appliances; tools; machines. We even see the countryside through their mediation: houses; streets; roads; paths; an avenue; a field; meadows; a civic wood. Manufactured things, man-made affairs or artificial social situations are our main partners in the majority of everyday events, especially work related ones. However, a relation to something natural is in fact an aspect of our daily living: the weather, for instance, reaches into our everyday world, and this has, even in its changeability, a certain typical order. Likewise with changes in the surrounding moods of our community and family and so forth—these also have their customary order. A relationship with the natural lives alongside our daily concerns as an intimate area or as an aspect of "the festive"—in the appearance of a free day or other free time. It is precisely such "freeness of time" like this which opens up possibilities for us of different dimensions of the world: the possibility of boredom; or the possibility of an outing into a different setting, whether a different landscape or different society; or even the possibility of an actual festivity.

Extraordinary situations open up extraordinary dimensions of some ordinary things, concerns and events; they point towards their natures and to our natures. An opportunity for such an opening up could be a holiday, by whose mediation we notice the yearly cycle of nature or society, and even the larger cycle of the progress of human life. Any unusual or otherwise extraordinary event could present a similar opportunity: an exceptional swing of the weather, by whose mediation we experience our exposure to the run of nature; an extraordinary social or personal event, whether happy or sad. Perhaps most typically, extraordinary situations arise simply: through a sudden, momentary liberation from everyday responsibilities; through the liberal living-through of freedom or opened-up possibilities.

The zone of ordinary overlaps with the extraordinary; our local surroundings refer to the wider world. They point to the world through spatial references (beyond the garden fence, beyond borders, looking at the sky), through temporal references (life-forming events), and interior references (the intimacy of body and thought). Our personal consciousness and social culture has to somehow reconcile itself with the relationship between the everyday and the extraordinary; it has to somehow cater for its establishing of normality inside the being of the world. Opportunities for such reconciliation used to be based in religion, that is, the cultural grasping of a religious experience of the world and life. However, the everyday and the extraordinary do not interrelate only at the edges. The extraordinary is not merely "elsewhere" or "another time" (in the most extreme case in the "afterlife"). The world is the background of every ordinary thing or event as long as it's revealed to us extraordinarily, that is, religiously or intimately, poetically or philosophically. But these various unveilings of the world can be conflicting, as in fact can various disclosures which are of the same order—say various religious ones, or from various schools of philosophy. The world shows itself in every nature, but nature is far from unambiguous. It's only made so once grasped as a thing by a different nature (ours for instance), and the method of this reification then expresses the character of what we know as "our world."

Each of us has our "own" kind of "world": our own way of perceiving, thinking and acting; our own environment where we feel at home, where we understand our surroundings and know how to act. But we know that homes of others exist as well, that beyond the borders of our own area the world can look different (in a neighbor's house for instance). We know that we can never be entirely sure of which way the borders of otherness run, for we only recognize that we've crossed them by the otherness which we encounter there—one which we don't always know how to deal with. We can easily get into situations where our existing abilities of orientation do not provide sufficient orientation and where our usual powers of action are ineffective.[12] We know that our area is finite, that it has an "otherwise" and an "elsewhere," a "before" and an "after."

---

12 See Miroslav Petříček jr.'s 1992–93 lecture course at the Faculty of Philosophy in the Charles University, "*O hranici*, na motivy Deleuzovy *Rhizomy*" [*Of the Border*, in the vein of Deleuze's *Rhizome*].

Our usual environment shares many of the characteristics of the world. It's the horizon of the phenomena we encounter in it; it's the context for our experiences, imagination and thought. Simultaneously, however, something of the "worldliness" of the world is missing in our usual environment. With a little discernment we recognize that our area is merely a part of the world, and not one just in the spatial sense. It's a kind of closest layer of links within the world that surrounds us, a nearest horizon. We share a large part of our area with other people, and usually also with some animals, trees, rivers or cliffs. The expression of such a human community is a common language, which also, of course, has many layers, from the common idiolects of a group of friends or colleagues, to usual speech patterns in certain situations and in certain strata of society, to dialects and the written national language. One can talk similarly about one's living environment, that is, about the nearest world horizon of family, group, stratum, region, nation and type of human culture. Every such environment is somehow a world for us, but simultaneously something is missing from them; they can refer back to a different one. Every such environment can link us to the world, but it can also isolate us from the world.

We can relate to the world through our surroundings and through the surroundings of those surroundings. But the world does not open itself up to us merely by our passing gradually along a path through a continually widening environment—even less so by a progressive tour of all thinkable, or at least all realizable, environments, or types of world, i. e., by our becoming polyglots and globalized cosmopolitans, whom nothing can surprise, at least as long as we remain in the globalized stratum of the world, wherever that may be. The world will not open up when we try to force the properties of our area upon it, when we extrapolate normality beyond its usual boundaries, or when we master the world with one "worldwide" language or culture. By doing so, we achieve nothing more than an expansion of the reach of ordinariness and an expansion of communicative space, which can be advantageous—and in this way alone sometimes contribute to the opening up of the world. We can, however, become actual citizens of the world—"cosmopolitans" in the philosophical sense of the word—in every disclosure that reveals the insufficiency of any environment, that is, in every natural relationship. Indeed, this is possible even in an encounter with a single nature that has already been experienced as a thing in one determined area, and all of this in one language. Yet the experience of other things, other environments and other languages or speech patterns, prepares us for this, at least as long as we don't confuse this experience for a simple collection of useful or exotic othernesses.

To describe the everyday environment that customarily represents our world, twentieth-century philosophy often uses the German term *Umwelt* (Jakob von Uexküll), "surrounding world." One advantage of this term is its biological connotations. As Petr Kouba explains,

> It is difficult to find a precise translation of the concept itself of Umwelt, and we do not intend here even to try. Nevertheless, Umwelt is equivalent to the personal world of a certain biological organism, its own living environment. Since every species of living creature has a specific way of interacting with its surroundings, in which certain structures of perceiving and behavior are realized, von Uexküll can distinguish specific worlds which connect to one or another species of living creature.[13]

We're capable of mentally situating individual people, a certain group, or cultural type into a customary environment, into their customary relations to the world and to inner experience. Some of these "surrounding worlds" (or "world surroundings") endeavor to expand successfully, to obscure the world, to conceal their own insufficiency in the face of the plurality of the world. Sometimes for a family this could be the "world" of the authoritative father; for a community it could be the "world" of a powerful individual; for a continent the "world" of a certain nation; or for the planet the "world" of a certain cultural type. Our broader environment is founded on just such contests between our narrower environments. The natural world, however, precedes all of this. It shows itself in such struggles, but is usually also devastated by them.

Humans have ambitions to be world beings, but this is not straightforward for them. Indeed it's an arduous task. It's a philosophical or sacral imposition, not a given condition and not in the least a call for expansion. Rather, it's a Heraclitean requirement for awakening. In their everydayness humans are merely beings of a certain area. For this reason, the older philosophic tradition, which was inspired by religion, talks of humans as neighbors in the world, whilst it reserves genuine "world citizenship" for God. This is despite the fact that in relation to the world the same tradition sees the human task as analogous to a unification with

---

13   Petr Kouba, *Světy a mezisvěty* [*Worlds and Between-Worlds*] (Prague: CTS UK, 2005).

God.[14] The universalism of monotheistic religions and philosophy is based on a parallel between itself and the uniqueness of a human being (of oneself), which is a task and not a given condition. Such a universalism can of course capsize and be confused for the expansion of certain visions of the world. Other inspirations to universalism can similarly be overturned, regardless of whether they are humanistic, scientific or atheist. Indeed, in making a rational reference to a more holistic world into ideology, the "world-view" is formed, which seemingly captures the holistic aspect of the world by consciously trying to replace the world with a construct, a whole with a synoptic artificial Umwelt.

In particular, it's possible to term the modern epoch, the "age of the world-view," as Martin Heidegger has done. The world-view confuses a unifying image of the world for the world itself. The world-view doesn't know the plurality of the world; indeed, it even simplifies the mutual relations of the horizons of the world in an effort to transpose them onto a single horizon. It's relatively unimportant whether what is concerned is the so-called "Christian world-view" or the "scientific world-view," also known as "scientific atheism." The world-view presents the delusion that we have found the only correct, or at least the most correct method of grasping nature. The world-view represents the delusion that things are not reified only at the point of a reifying grasp of nature, but that they are already at our disposal as objects, that they simply occur so. It's the delusion that we can reify even the very structure of the world, that the structure of the world presents itself to us as objective.

The world-view pretends that the medium by which a certain spiritual current (science or religion) becomes ideology is the world, which unproblematically anchors each of our normalities into a relationship with the whole. It is precisely in this that every world-view differs from the religious experience of "something else" and from the thinker's ethos of impartial enquiry. The world-view offers a certain explanation of matter, space, and time, as well as of the knowability of the world, and sometimes even of the meaning of life. Many of these explanations originally belong to basic sacral, philosophical or scientific discoveries, but in the world-view they are rid of their problematic and thus life-giving natural contexts, becoming pieces of a web constructed from only one point of view. Such pragmatic approaches to the world are

---

14 This is the case, for instance, with the Hellenized Jewish thinker Philon of Alexandria at around the beginning of the Christian calendar, for whom a human is *paroikos*, "a neighbour," whereas God is *kosmou polites*. *De Cherubim* 34.

so typical for modernity that we often cannot conceive science or even religion in another way, that is, as inherent in the world of natural experience.

The world-view rids us of responsibility for a way of experiencing the world; it seems enough just to decide on the "correct" world-view. In the worst-case scenario, one person would choose the atheist, another the Creationist. However, through this the world-view isolates us considerably from natural experience. This is because those components of natural experience that are too "heretical" pass through the filter of the world-view's automatic censoring of consciousness only sporadically, and it is not afterwards at all clear how they fit together. They do not form a natural world, but rather a problematical remainder or addendum, for whose grasp we don't have sufficiently cultural means. And so this remaining experience of natural being is usually grasped by notably obscure methods, the so-called "alternative" ones.

The world-view simplifies our perception of the world, and by this it empowers us with direct exterior action. The man of the world-view does not pose himself questions, but solves problems. This relates not only to modern technological sciences, which give the impression that one day all human problems will be solved by technology, but also to the spread of the modern world-view from Europe across the whole planet, alternately in the names of faith, scientific enlightenment, well-being and gain. Sometimes this is economic gain; at others it's a gain in rationality or in a projected afterlife. The world-view is quotidian thinking; it represents the expansion of the ordinary into the realm of the extraordinary, an expansion of one-track uniformity and all encompassing homogeneity. It is the expansion of everyday thought into extraordinary values, whether they are those of religion, philosophy or science. This irresponsible distension of normality in the name of apparent utility and surveyability devastates the world, and does so both in the devastation of the nature on planet Earth, and in the devastation of social structures, our thinking, perception and language. The reaction to these devastations, or also the reaction to the reciprocal conflict between world-views (where there are similar devastating trends) can then be seen as a typically postmodern crumbling of the world, a "withdrawal of the world." Every environment, every nearest horizon of the world is then granted independence, but it is somehow unbecoming, even almost impossible, to discuss mutual references. The area of everydayness, which no longer refers to the wider world, ceases being synoptic. From the modern desire to secure ourselves in the totality of the world through its overall

surveyability, we arrive at the insecure homelessness of our newly fragmentary postmodern everyday.

Is our search for the natural world in this situation not then somewhat old fashioned? Isn't it just another attempt at maintaining an old
universalism, merely in a particularly complicated form? Studying the
difficulties of deliberations over the natural world in the twentieth century adds gravity to such questions. After all, Edmund Husserl had to
revise his conception of phenomenology. The study investigating exactly
the immediately given became, after the abandonment of the concept
Phänomenologie als strenge Wissenschaft (Phenomenology as Hard Science),
more of a method capable of disclosing ever more original relationships.
In his later meditations about the world, Martin Heidegger substantially
changed the concept of thought from the period of *Sein und Zeit*, for-
merly based on the analysis of everyday concerns and dealings in things.
And Jan Patočka also returned several times to his habilitation work
*Přirozený svět jako filosofický problém (The Natural World as a Philosophical
Problem)*.[15] In spite of all of these problems, phenomenology pointed
out the now already classic route of late modern thinking back towards
direct and natural experience. However, this does not mean that we
shouldn't search for other, and perhaps more appropriate routes.

In Husserl's writings, we encounter the expression "natural world,"
or rather "life-world" (*Lebenswelt*), in direct connection with the exposition of phenomenological reduction, *epoche*, by the help of which we are
to return to before the world of science and then even to before the world
of everyday experience.

> If our interest is exclusively in the "life-world," we must ask: Has the life-
> world, through the epoche in respect to objective science, already been
> laid open as a universal scientific subject matter? . . . How do we have
> the life-world as a universal field, fixed in advance, of such establishable
> facts?[16]

Epoche is a Greek word introduced into philosophy in the second
century BC by the skeptic Carneades as an expression for "abstention

---

15 Prague 1936, 1970, 1992. In the second edition there is an extended appendix *Přirozený svět
   v meditaci svého autora po třiceti letech* [*The natural world in the meditations of its author after
   thirty years*]. The last critical review comes from the postscript to the French edition published in 1976.

16 Husserl, *Crisis*, 137–8.

from agreement." For Husserl it is firstly a withholding agreement with the consequences of the progress of objective sciences, which veil our natural living world. The motivation for *epoche* is not an anti-scientific orientation—Husserl himself was a mathematician—but rather an attempt at disclosing the pre-scientific foundation for the world of experience, which could also be the foundation of science. The natural world of our life, however, has not shown itself to be an apt theme for science. In the depths of its nature and animation it does not provide unambiguous "establishable facts," it is not in a "universal field, fixed in advance." In its everyday dimension, the world of our lives offers a sufficiency of facts for a possible exploration, but their truth is relative to their cultural contexts. Husserl elaborates the term *epoche*: *epoche* no longer withholds only its agreement from expositions of the world made by objective science; it is not only a reduction from science, but also a reduction from the world. "Transcendental *epoche* (transcendental reduction)" withholds each single agreement that we make with every commonplace when it places "general thesis of the world" in parentheses. *Epoche* does not contend the existence of the world, it merely "parenthesizes" it. We try to give evidence about the phenomena of unmediated experience, and this is made possible precisely by withholding every preceding judgment about the world, every preceding assumption about probable associations. The vacant judgment should be based on the obvious and not presumptively based on a certain theory about the character of the world. Parenthesizing every theory of the world is the way towards continually disclosing ever more primal experiences. But can it ever show a "primary" ("innate") web of relations and horizons?

Phenomenological reduction (transcendental *epoche*) is a reduction of a diametrically opposed type to that of modern scientific knowledge. *Epoche* refers in the opposite direction to that of the scientific reductive method, pointing towards the subjectivity of experience. Reduction in the sense of objective scientific knowledge represents an extreme and reifying grasping of nature, usually by the translation of experiences ("secondary qualities") into some quantity. A phenomenologist's *epoche* represents nature in the depths of subjectivity. Thereby, of course, it exposes itself to all the problems of the modern philosophy of transcendental subjectivity. We are rid of all the presumptions that have grown out of modern metaphysics with the exception of its founding thought, that is, the thought of transcendental consciousness, of the structure *ego cogito cogitatum*. This problem will manifest itself also in the difficulties of thinking about corporeality and intersubjectivity.[17]

Heidegger's departure from the modern ontology of the subject leads firstly to skepticism regarding the possibility of approaching the natural world. His alternative, in *Sein und Zeit*, is an analysis of everyday concerns, the handling of things. "The worldliness of the world" shows itself only as a whole of sufficiency. If we disregard Heidegger's later changes of thinking, this approach meets with Fink's criticism: Does the being of a thing exhaust itself through being taken for a useful thing? Is utility itself unambiguous?[18] After all, mediation conceals aims. Admittedly, a "thing" is that which is required, which is for a purpose, as the Greek term for "thing," *chrema*, already expressed, i.e., a necessary something. A thing can, however, also be experienced abnormally, festively. Even useful things can become transparent and reveal being. In addition, things can be genuine symbols. A thing does not have only the meaning conferred on it by humans, but fundamental human events cannot transpire without a place and without things. A thing also makes the world present.

The natural world is not only a philosophical problem, but also a problem of life. Is not the natural world after all, a world of mythopoeic experience, of the immediacy of a child, ignorant of distant horizons, the past and the future? Isn't it a world of dreamlike experiences, those of an unwoken consciousness? If so, our task could scarcely be that of entering and remaining in the natural world. Philosophy's work would then be more of an interpreting of this state after waking from it; it would be an intermediary between this state and objective knowledge. In such a case, the philosophy of nature would refer more to philosophizing about myth, or through depth psychology to the unconscious. It would be an attempt at mediating between childish or oneiric experience, and scientific or even technological knowledge. The philosophy of nature undoubtedly possesses this role and it is an important role. Our theory, however, is that the task of the philosophy of nature is greater, more fundamental, and also more active.

What then is the "natural world"? First of all, it is no "something," not even an open field for the occurrence of something or things. The natural world is a life-long problem. It is not the risk of betting on one or another explanation of the world or world-view, but rather a problem of

---

17 See "Das Problem der Einfühlung", fragments of manuscripts by E. Husserl from 1934, in *Zur Phänomenologie der Intersubjektivität*, edited by Iso Kern (Springer: Dordrecht, 1973).

18 Eugen Fink, *Existenz und Co-Existenz* (Würzburg: Königshausen und Neumann, 1987).

continually discovering sense—a problem of encountering, apprehending, interpreting and acting. The natural world shows itself as a demand for understanding other or new perspectives, experiences and views. It manifests itself in the demand and in the opportunity for experiencing the ordinary extraordinarily; in the possibility and requirement of interpreting the surrounding world of other people or other cultures; in the demand and opportunity for orienting oneself in a situation that has no precedent, or at least, orienting oneself not only from the perspective of something which is generally applicable.

The problem of the natural world is not just a problem of philosophy and of nature, but it's also a different expression of the problem of the constitution of human identity. For the problem of the natural world is one of self-discovery through the world. The unity of the natural world in the plurality of its possibilities, claims, and possible expositions is apparently correlative with the unity of a human being in the plurality of his or her possibilities and changes, although it is worthless trying to decide on what is the "cause" of what here. The unity of a human being and the unity of the world are a task we won't scale by a short-cut solution prescribing the unity of the world or a human being from one perspective. Every such short-cut approach devastates the world and the person; it devastates nature.

Some human possibilities are in perception, in meeting each other, understanding, and acting. Freedom is also present in this understanding, interpretation, and plurality of possible reasonable explanations. The natural world can be a task of consciousness, a work of pluralist open unity. We will not prevent the devastation of nature by a mere regression to the very beginning, but rather with a new way of performing consciousness, a disclosure of the freedom of the soul's movement, the freedom of life movement. What is needed is an unveiling of the freedom of "being between" diverse individual explanations of the world, between surrounding "worlds"; a disclosure of being as interpretation loyal to the nature which it interprets, and which is so precisely because it appreciates its polysemy.

This view of the character of the natural world can meet with the criticism that what is concerned is not a natural world, but a cultural one, an artificial one formed by a human interpretative feat. But what could be more natural—that is, what could be closer to *physis*—than interpretation, than searching for the possibilities of expression and meaning? The conservation of past manifestations of *physis* is not natural. But it is natural to search for new possibilities of forms when the search is in permanent contact with the sources of these possibilities. A natural culture is one that makes real the possibilities of *physis* and looks after the field of germination. Culture is part of the nature of a human being, but at the same time it always exposes human nature to the risk of damage through auto-domestication.

5. Matter in experience, philosophy and science. Metaphysical explanations of matter. The intuition of the material and corporeal. The devastation of nature and the world as a consequence of the devastation of the meaning of matter

The world shows itself to us in every nature and in the connections between natures, in how the natural shows itself in the world. We interpret a certain dimension of a given nature through grasping this nature as a thing, and we do so in the frame of a certain understanding of the world. Every perceived or imagined thing carries the seal of our interpretation of the world. We cannot however, ever reify the world itself entirely. Somehow we can perceive and think the references of connections and horizons, but as relations of sense we are only able to amazedly interpret them rather than firmly grasp them. Nature eludes our reification by its polysemy and its metamorphic quality. But the world is so far wide of every possible reification, that every grasping of it is already a mere imitation of the world, one of many possible images of the relations between natures. Despite this, we try, in order to orient ourselves in the world, to grasp some of the framing relations of natures, to grasp some dimensions of the world. We struggle for a grasp of what founds our experience as somehow comprehendible, for an understanding of how natures arise in our experience. In asking about the world in this way, we're actually asking about the frames of our understanding of natures, even when we talk of various possible interpretations of the world.

The tradition of European thought, as it appears in philosophy and in science, foregrounds a number of basic frames for our perception and understanding. Of these, matter, space, and time have their own prominent place. Matter, space, and time are such fundamental frames for our perceiving and grasping of natures that every reification of *physis* is, at the same time, based on some understanding of them. The modern interpretation of the world, which reduces the relations of sense to quantitative relations of significations, is rooted in one reductive explanation of matter, space, and time.

Things will only present themselves to us in certain situations, that is, in space and in time—and they present themselves as material things. Indeed, the mass of a thing is an important indication that we are dealing with a thing that is a grasped nature, and not with a mere image, figment of the imagination, or purely formal (mathematical or logical) object. There are in fact many real things that I can touch or grasp in the literal and original sense of the word. It's true that I cannot touch some, not being able to reach them when they are too far, or too small or big. Some things it's also not always wise to touch, say a viper or a naked flame. Nevertheless we sense that it would somehow be possible to touch these, and that the problem is really a question of abilities. Some natures seem to dodge from under our fingers, either because they're insufficiently firm to be gripped, or because they don't have a marked out or solidified shape: as with air, water, or frogspawn. But the difficulties of grasping these are of a very different character to the essential troubles with grasping an image in a mirror, Pythagoras' theorem, or the million crowns I won in a dream. I can think even things like these—very well in fact in the case of Pythagoras' theorem—but I cannot examine them with my hands. A reasonable person will deal with these things differently than with material things. So, for example, it is not necessary to regularly clean Pythagoras' theorem; it is better to understand it, a task that is not even particularly difficult.

For our everyday perceiving and understanding, matter is the criterion of reality. Materiality is that symptom of natural being, which is neither just a reflection of something else, nor a mere formality, fiction, or figment. Materiality pertains to that which has emerged in actuality—which on the everyday level is a reflection of nature, of what, in other words, has been born. Matter is, in a sense, reliable, most probably precisely because of its naturalness or its independence, i.e., its less than total reliance on us. Even an artificially manufactured thing is actual in that its manufacture respects the properties of the fabric. We have acquired the habit in modernity, of calling this independence from us "objectivity." The Latin word *obiectum* means "that, which is thrown before" or "obstacle"; that which stops our hands or breaks our ideas; that which clashes with our will. While on the one hand, this distinctly relates to shape, and hence to a spatial aspect, it also relates to matter.

Matter for us is something firm in its reliability and weightiness. We can rationalize it as an impenetrability, as inertia, as heaviness. These dimensions of heaviness and difficulty are also the dominant signatures of reality for us, of whatever we need to hold our own in, and in which things are laboriously born and actualized. The thought and action we now regard as realistic in ordinary life take seriously not only this firmness and reliability, but also the weightiness and often the injuring hardness of matter as well. The realism of the everyday is a different one than the scholastic realism of ideas or general conceptions. It is the realism of bodily humanity and the relation to material things.

Of course, realistic thought and action take other properties of many material things seriously as well. Take, for instance, the fact that some material things evade us through being fluid. This elusiveness can be pleasant, and for this reason many people enjoy swimming, but it can also be unpleasant, like the feel of slime. It can soften the hardness of matter, but it can also be deceiving, for "still waters run deep." It can surprise; it can bring but also take away. Just as the hardness of matter refers to a shape and hence to something spatial, so its fluidity refers to elusiveness and hence to something temporal, something time-bound. Fluidity is part of material life, letting us taste both its wealth and its poverty. It enriches the firm side of matter, but it also exposes its meagerness, although it does so differently to the way it is exposed by hardness, since it manifests transience. Everything material is transient.

Everyday life tries to enjoy transience and elusiveness, but simultaneously it wants to secure itself in the solid, to lean on the permanent. It wants to benefit from flux and at the same time be anchored in certainty. This certainty is, through the mediation of the firm (shape-related) side of matter, offered by knowledge, or at least by an institution—whether legal, financial, ecclesiastical, or one for insurance. Thus everyday life attempts amidst matter to enjoy time, and simultaneously to outflank it, or at least do so a little through the mediation of the spatial dimensions of matter or through the mediation of thought. All of this legitimately belongs to our normality.

Our experience however is not only always ordinary. Sometimes we experience and think extraordinarily; sometimes we succeed in being present when nature is in action, that is, we succeed in actually existing in the disclosure of some power of nature. Occasionally we're capable of wonder, from which piety, poetry, philosophy or science can sprout. Are we however, capable of experiencing matter extraordinarily? After all, matter is practically a symptom of ordinariness itself.

Facets of extraordinary experiences of matter are the spontaneity of material nature, the elemental force, the intimacy of corporeality, and the intuitive charge of feeling, tasting, and smelling. However, one of the features of an objectifying grasp is that it tries to think about the extraordinary in an ordinary way. And so something as close to our nature as matter becomes something customary, weighable even. The spontaneity of matter escapes the rational side of our everyday thinking, as it does with most philosophical or scientific thought.

The mind feels itself to be weighed down and limited by matter. The mind comprehends the extraordinary more in the context of a liberation from matter, weight, and corporeality; it prefers to grasp the extraordinary as something spiritual. In European thought, "matter and spirit" make a direct proverbial dichotomy, despite the fact that a part of the opposition between them has more to do with notions of space. The antagonism between matter and spirit as well as the confusion of matter for something that takes up space, culminates in philosophy and in the science of classic modernity. Descartes defines the spirit (soul, mind) as *res cogitans*, the "thinking thing." Everything else, that is, everything substantial, he defines as *res extensa*, the "extended thing." When the connection between the body and soul is understood in this way, the body becomes a space for the action of the soul, its instrument and its source of problems. Living or non-living material bodies are comprehended and explained as mechanisms, in which matter is merely their fabric. The mechanical explanation of the world separates us from the intuition of matter. Matter is reduced to a stuffing for bodily things, and spontaneity is perceived only as a course of events in the realm of the spirit—if it is perceived at all. This view can then be inverted: it is possible to declare only the stuffing as real, and consciousness as simply its expression, ostensible or at least secondary. "What came first, matter or spirit?" It's not only at our latitude that this late modern pseudo-philosophical question is still asked. The answer "matter" is labeled as "materialism," whilst the answer "spirit" as "idealism." Applied to the majority of modern thought, this question makes some sense. Its pseudo-philosophical status lies "only" in that it attempts to be a global question, an arbitrator for all the thoughts and experiences of various times and cultures. This, by the way, is the destiny of more than one "ism." Furthermore, it is reminiscent of another well-known question: "What came first, the chicken or the egg?" One cannot therefore neglect to mention the words of the original Czech thinker Jiří Němec: "Materialists muddle up matter with materials; idealists think that what they've thought up actually exists."

There has, however, been something awkward about attempts to think about matter ever since the beginning of philosophy. Although the term "matter" is pre-philosophic, used in the Homeric epics and the lyrics of Alcman, surprisingly it isn't found in the pre-Socratics, including those who tend to be classified later among the "materialists." Similarly, it's difficult to find an expression for "body" in their writing. In philosophy, matter becomes a theme at the beginning of the late classical period. For Plato, matter (*hyle*) is more of an opportunity for phenomena, and it relates closely to space. Linked to this is a low valuation of human corporeality, which is a common problem in antiquity, amplified also by the influence of the "Orphic" conception of a bodily birth as a fall of the soul from the realm of the gods, for "we came under this roofed cave . . ." (already in Empedocles B120, if Porphyry can be trusted). In Aristotle, matter is the potentiality (*dynamis*) of existence, whilst its actuality (*energeia*) functions as an essential shape (*morphe*). As a potentiality, matter for him is eternal. When he refers to the pre-Socratic thinkers, it sounds sometimes almost like an indictment for "materialism."

> Of the first philosophers, then, most thought that the principles (*archai*) which were of the nature of matter (*hyle*) were the only principles of all things. That of which all things that are consist, the first from which they come to be, the last into which they are resolved (the substance remaining, but changing in its modifications), this they say is the element (*stoicheion*) and the principle (*arche*) of things (*to on*), and therefore they think that nothing is either generated or destroyed . . . Yet they do not all agree as to the number and the nature of these principles. Thales, the founder of this type of philosophy, says that the principle is water . . .[19]

Here we have the inception of a thousand years of misunderstanding for the pre-Socratics. It results from our assumption that their propositions are answers to the question "from which," and our subsequent contextualizing of these propositions using anachronistic conceptions. Thales surely was not so naïve as to think that everything is "from" water in the material sense—which furthermore a modern person would imagine as having been "made from" water. That, from which things "come to be," and "the last into which they are resolved" is not some fabric of those things. For Anaximander it is "*apeiron*, indeterminacy,

---

19 Aristotle, *Metaphysics* 1.3.983b. Thales A12. This translation is by W. D. Ross in *The Basic Works of Aristotle* (New York: Modern Library Classics, 2001), 693–4.

boundlessness," the possibility of differences (antagonisms) emerging, which determine everything singular as long as they have effect. Aristotle however, is not naïve at all when he understands the "from which" insinuated into the pre-Socratics as the "underlying" (*hypokeimenon*), which Cicero will go on to translate into Latin as *subiectum*. It is a reference to the unconscious spontaneity underlying *physis*, a subsoil for growth and emergence.

Neither is Aristotle naïve when defining matter himself. The determined matter of a thing that has a certain shape—say the material of a statue—is merely a simulacrum for matter and shape. So for instance, a statue is of marble, but marble is again a material thing, just less determined than a statue, less determined than marble of a precise shape. For Aristotle, philosophically-thought matter is indeterminacy itself, the potential of something. One cannot touch such matter. Primary matter is the limit of indeterminacy in shape; it's an ontological and not a mechanical component of material things. It is the potential for change in every nature. Primary matter cannot become the object of any science, since in itself it is no object. It will only become an object as "extendedness" in the Cartesian explanation of Suarez's metaphysics, which, for the first time will bestow matter with independent existence.

The ancient understanding of matter eludes not only late modern judges, who try everywhere to distinguish between "materialism" and "idealism." On the whole, it says little about our experience of material nature. Between us and antiquity lie a number of fundamental new experiences that transform our perception of matter: the Christian evaluation of corporeality as a sign of individuality; late antiquity's discovery of interiority; the later Renaissance experience of the independence of matter. Utterly paradoxical is the influence of the Christian message. On the one hand it values corporeality and individuality, even in the Christological and eschatological dogmas. On the other, it takes, in practice, an extremely hostile stance towards everything material and corporeal—hostile, that is, even by the standards of lingering antiquity, although only the Gnostics admit to this in their teachings.

The development of human perception and thinking in the last few millennia can, with a certain level of overstatement, be understood as a gradual manifestation of matter, corporeality, and individuality. Every experience of the world reveals itself as material—as comprehensive, or bodily. As a result, it is somehow reliable in spite of its individual placement. Matter shows itself as the subsoil (*hypokeimenon, subiectum*) of transformations of nature—of their coming to be and passing away—as an unapparent basis of individual existence. It shows itself as the possibility of shapes, the possibility of change, and in the inclination towards assuming shape. It reveals itself as the principle of multiplicity[20] for all individual and transient entities, as a source of multiplicity, in which the unity of the world is born. Matter also appears as the bodily depth of everything individual and transient, a depth whose surface I can occasionally touch, and which I can also sometimes experience from within.

Matter shows itself as a dimension of the world, as the permanence of the order of temporality. Every singular nature is, by its character, mutable and hence temporal, but the inexhaustibility of matter as "subsoil" and the depths of every nature make it possible for the order of the world to outreach in its permanence every individual nature. For this reason, every nature can appear to us as time-bound and the world as overarching all individual natures both in its constancy and in its possibilities. Everything material is transient, but it is just from the point-of-view of transience that matter appears as a permanent inner source.

As long as matter is experienced as a source of the unconquerable power of natures and as underlying their shapes, then it cannot be grasped itself. The reifying grasp of natures and our thought merely points towards matter as *apeiron*, *hypokeimenon*, or as Aristotle's "primary matter." Although pointing to matter in this way does help determine a method of grasping individual natures, and thereby a type of world (a certain understanding of the world), it does not grasp matter itself. Examples of attempts to grasp matter on this level of perception and thought are, for instance, a study of the elements, or alchemical practice. Such grasps of matter are not reifying. Neither an element, nor an alchemical substance is a thing; they are not at our everyday disposal. Instead, they point out the profound dynamic of matter—elementality and not reification. For this very reason, these attempts are not science in the modern sense of the word.

The beginning of modernity presented our thought with the task of apprehending new sensitivity for matter. For the thinkers of the late Renaissance, matter showed itself within the being of all individual transient things. However, the inherited remains of scholastic doctrine and the technical orientations of many early modern thinkers made it impossible to conceive of matter's new experiential claim otherwise than

---

20 Compare the scholastic doctrine *materia est principium individuationis*, "matter is the principle of individualisation," that is, the multiplication of that which is common in many material realisations. Examples could be many singular plants of the same species, or drawn circles.

by a new metaphysical grasp.[21] Matter began to be thought of as an entity. The traditionally metaphysical tendency to think of being as the greatest entity led to the postulate of the universal essence of matter, which was thus explained as the method of being of all individual tran-sient and bodily entities. Combined with the period's will for a radical simplification of "unnecessary" delicacies in traditional philosophical terminology, this produced the presumptions of modern science: the material unity of the world; the principle of inertia; the law of pres-ervation. Matter was understood as a homogenous and reliable filling for empty space in the outside world, which made possible a technically very effective mechanomorphic exposition of the world. The attempt at gaining a knowledge of matter now promised a general knowledge of the character of everything that was in the world. And modern science, particularly physics and chemistry, moved gradually towards realizing this possibility. Matter was also understood as *materia inertia*, that is, lazy or inert matter, filling in the extents of spatial forms. This made it possible to connect the conception of matter with a physical variable representing mass, and to introduce a physical unit for it. Its concrete value (1kg) was arbitrary. What was significant was the interconnection of matter, mass and any physical unit for it, as was the next step of estab-lishing the material equivalents of physical energy.

However, this exceptionally effective modern way of explaining the world is limited by its method of cognitive reduction. Based on the given philosophical presumptions of the scientific grasp of the world, it attempts to gain a knowledge of matter itself, but can only cognize in-dividual shapes, forms or arrangements of that which is material. We're continually learning about much that is material, but matter itself is always hiding "under" it, or "inside" it—perpetually running before our grasp. The grasping of science customarily forces this escaping matter into the realm of the very small, into ever-smaller domains of the mi-croworld. In the twentieth century, the attempt to shift the grasping of matter to the grasping of some of its basic shapes brought about a de-mand for a revision of traditionally modern presumptions concerning knowability. Matter thus ceased to be a passive filling for space in the outside world. Now, the traditionally modern reduction of matter to a filling for spatial extents no longer satisfies the natural sciences and even less so philosophical thought, in particular the kind that wants to be loyal to the original experiences of the new sensitivity for matter and

---

21   See Ivor Leclerc, *The Nature of Physical Existence* (London: Allen & Unwin, 1972).

corporeality. I can hardly view my own body only as an exterior spatial formation filled with matter-like stuffing structured in a definite, complicated way. Matter is surely something more interesting than just an opportunity for a spatial structure from the level of the microcosm up. Likewise, it's surely something more interesting than mere inertia, impassivity. It cannot only be a passive candidate waiting to be pushed or pulled. The classic modern grasp of the world failed to adopt into itself the experience of material corporeality.

One can grasp material things as objects. And so they can be objectively explored. But from the position of what subject do we do so? And is matter itself "objective"? Can the cognitive and experiencing subject be reduced to something "spiritual" or soul-related, and can matter be reduced to a filling for sets of objects? After all, matter is experienced as that which is underlying (i.e., the *subiectum* of) all natures and all life, and this is how it was also conceived.

Nature shows itself in the tension between its possibilities; it emerges from the relationship between spontaneity and the possession of shape. A material thing arises in the encounter between the spontaneity of matter and a noticeable shape, in a meeting that always has a certain character, that is, the character of a world event. Such an interpretation of the Platonic and Aristotelean teachings about things as constituted by matter and shape (hylemorphic teachings) show a thing as the boundary between the unconscious spontaneity of matter and a shape that is graspable through consciousness. It represents the world as a mode of establishing relationships between the unconscious and the conscious. Material nature mutates, but its discovery and its grasping as a thing always occurs in one of its definite likenesses and this likeness is an aspect of the style of the world, one which consolidates our experience and makes explanations of it possible. Even our own human corporeality shows itself to be a certain way of connecting to the unconscious, to that which shows itself in consciousness as both weight and firmness yet also, at the same time, a source of mutability, growth, and transience. Matter is the medium for actualizing. A theological hymn from the beginning of the twentieth century states: "If we are ever to possess you, having taken you rapturously in our arms, we must then go on to sublimate you through sorrow. . ." [22]

---

22   Pierre Teilhard de Chardin, "The Spiritual Power of Matter," in *Hymn of the Universe* (New York: Harper and Row, 1961).

The devastation of inner nature is, to the greatest extent, a devastation of matter. A departure from an intrinsic intuition of matter is a departure from nature in our perception, thinking and acting. The modern world is characterized precisely by matter thought of only as an inert filling for some prefabricated parts. In such a world, evolution came as a big surprise, and an even bigger surprise was the spontaneity of individuals and human society, which does not fit into deterministically prescribed ends.

Nature is devastated by every devastation of matter, whether it is materialistic or idealistic. For neither of these allow for a moment of respect in the intuition of matter. Both value "tasting" less than "seeing." But what, in this situation, could represent a natural way of caring for matter, for the experience of the material, of the natural?

An attempt to answer the question about caring for the material world leads us to a central theme in depth psychology, namely, the problematics of the relationship between the conscious and unconscious. A pride or fear of consciousness, which cloisters itself from unconscious requirements and inspirations, leads to sterility in consciousness and later to a shock. Only a careful and demanding cultivation of everything that arises from the unconscious allows individuation, an actualization of the conscious claim for unity. A natural unity is laboriously born in life's contest, whilst a totalitarian imitation of singularity can simply be declared. Since we can oversee neither the possibilities nor the demands of matter, we have nothing left other than to turn our searching towards clearer, more expressible regions, and we do so trying not to weaken our fundamental intuition that what is material is real.

6. The structuring of space. Space and the world. Shape—*eidos, morphe*. Shape and categories of natural kinds (*eidos* = species). Shape and knowability. The fumbling of shape (kind) in trying to find itself, and shaping space. Landscape and orientation. A map. The devastation of space

We come to know and to grasp any nature through its characteristic shape. Every nature contends for its shape, is an opportunity for the emergence of certain shapes. Every nature not only fights for its space by taking up a certain area, but primarily by structuring its inner and its surrounding space. No nature can be imagined without its space, that is, without a certain structure of connections and opportunities. Every nature stands out from its setting in the way it actualizes its possibilities—and with each such actualization it transforms also the layout of its own future possibilities and that of many other natures. Every coalescence into shape from within the environment is simultaneously a drawing of boundaries, by the mediation of which nature communicates with its surroundings: it follows the character of its surroundings and also affects the structure of its surroundings. Examples could be crystallization for instance, or the growth of a tree. This occurs similarly also on the level of thinking and speech: every addition to a text changes the possibilities of future additions, and changes also the external associations of the text, its relation to other texts say, or the relation it bears to certain types of reader and to certain types of interpretation. And again, interpretations of texts or thoughts behave similarly; they grasp at a certain meaning in the interpreted, complete it, and change its relations to other interpretations and to other themes of interpretation. This applies not just to interpretations of a text, but also to all reifying grasps of nature, since they are always explanations or understandings. Such connections are an aspect of every nature's being a being in the world.

The world opens up to us as a space of possibilities and actualizations, as a space for sharing and for individualization. Every nature surfaces from indeterminacy through the structure of possibilities of the world into which it enters. And by this process of becoming extrinsic, every nature enriches the world: not just with a new thing to be grasped, but also by reaching into the holistic structure of the world as a space of connections. Indeed, quite often we talk of the world as we would about a space. What is concerned is the possibility of shapes emerging, the possibility of changes, the possibility of something definite as well as that of transformations; it is a field of relations between the fixed and the flexible. The ancients talked of the "harmony of the world" with this sense in mind—about the coupling of the definiteness of the grasped and the indefiniteness of the mutable. Thanks to the space of the world and its structure, shapes can arise that we can grasp. Can we, however, grasp space itself? Wouldn't this attempt be as shoreless as the attempt to grasp matter, which always escapes our comprehension into depths far from consciousness? Or might space offer some detectable structures of the natural world?

Space is in the world; space is a possibility of worldly being. Every grasp of nature is also a certain interpretation of space to which that nature belongs—and by this token it is also part of an interpretation of the world. The attempt of a world-view to grasp the world as a whole is, at the same time, an attempt to exhaust space with one explanation of it. Probably the most widespread notion of this sort is the conception of space as an empty reservoir without walls. Things occur as objects that fill up part of this space without influencing in any way its properties. The occurrence of objects in such a space is limited only by their material aspect, that is, their impassability, for two material objects cannot, in a world explained in this way, take up the same place—they wouldn't fit. In this kind of space, a place is something apriori and absolute; it is independent of any of its actualizations. For this reason all places are equivalent in space. Relatedly, this space must be both of an absolute size (i.e., actually endless), and equivalent in all directions. Otherwise privileged places would arise, whether related to boundaries or centers. Space grasped in this way has one very useful property in practice: it is linear. Every distance can be transposed using a quantity of a simple character (a scalar). This conception of space is also practically useful because it can be understood as emptiness which is, here and there, filled in with matter, material objects which occur in such space. Space is then the vacant opportunity for occurrence, and matter is the filling of a place (the place of the occurrence of an object). Matter does not affect space in any other way than by taking up room. Such an understanding is ideal for the easy construction of mechanisms and for a mechanistic exposition of the world. It does not, however, allow for any nature. This is because it can't accommodate any other kind of change than a change of place (position) and because there is no opportunity in it for interactions other than the reciprocal knocking of neighboring objects.

The mechanistic grasp of space is illustrative because in it a shape is only a taking-up of space. It's also illustrative because of how it ties on to a certain explanation of ancient atomism, for which space is a void, and hence, a nonentity that also somehow is, that is, precisely as emptiness. An actual entity that *is* is then that which occurs in such a space, and it must be discrete and inherently unified and immutable, hence it has to be some kind of little piece of actuality itself, moving around in absolute emptiness without properties. Unlike ancient atomism however, these little pieces also push against each other. By grasping space as emptiness, nature is reduced to the mechanical movement of some basic actuality, to a movement of solid bodies or material points in a given space. The world is reduced to a machine, one that also has the character of an occurrence.

The natural world, however, does not have the character of an occurrence, nor can it be exhausted with one grasping interpretation. The world of natures can be perceived in various ways and also thought of in various ways, but space always goes with it. The character of the space of the world is related to the method by which natures are grasped. Without space we would have nothing to grasp, or how, for we would have no opportunity for doing so. Certain grasps outline certain types of space as the structures of certain interpretations of the world. In this way, one can, in our context, arguably explain Kant's definition of space and time as apriori forms.

The mathematician,[23] physicist, or biologist[24] will find opportunities for various interpretations of space in the world of natures in their own disciplines. The history of philosophy, however, offers us the oldest attempt at explaining the relationship between space and shape. We encounter it in Plato's dialogue, the *Timaeus*. The problem is how and

---

23 See Petr Vopěnka, "Neviditelné reálné tvary" ["Invisible real shapes"] in *Geometrie živého* [*Geometry of the Living*] (Prague: Doporučená četba, 1991), 35.

24 See Zdeněk Neubauer "O strukturalistickém hnutí v biologii" ["About the Structuralist Movement in Biology"] in *Geometrie živého* [*Geometry of the Living*] (Prague: Doporučená četba, 1991), 43.

where ideas act as perceivable shapes. What, next to ideas, is the basis of the potential for appearance and perception—that is, what gives every individual nature the potential for growth and change? Plato suggests the possibility of a phenomenal existence that can be understood as matter. He does so particularly in terms of the traditional elemental conception of nature, but the notion can also be compared to memory[25], or alternatively, explained as spatial possibility.

In the *Timaeus*, the possibility of the existence of phenomena is termed *tithene*,[26] thus "suggesting" or "setting up" (derived from the verb *tithenai*). Shortly before in the dialogue there was talk about this suggesting or setting up as a "persuading," *peithein*.[27] This is not just any kind of persuading, but the creative cosmogenic effect of the mind (*nus*) on necessity (*ananke*), thanks to which necessity allows the emergence of something apparent, that is, of an individual nature. The mind persuades necessity to step aside and allow formation or transformation, and it persuades it by offering—"suggesting"—an idea (view, shape), or in other words, something that necessity can consent to, but which simultaneously opens up a new opportunity. This persuading and suggesting opens a new space; it opens up a degree of freedom in the worldly being of phenomena. The result of this persuasion is a glimpsable shape, which can, by way of hints, become real through the development of a certain apparent nature, and which simultaneously makes it possible for this nature to be grasped, distinguished, and incorporated into an order of thinking. The mind offers necessity a spatial ordering that does not lead to contradiction, and does so both in the area of pure geometry and from perspectives of logical spaces, spaces of configurations, and others. This contradiction-free solution to the birth of nature is *eidos* (idea, shape, species). Intuition gains a possible insight and necessity gives way to it. Through necessity's giving way thus, a certain type of space is established, which is determined precisely by what necessity gave way to, namely, that for which there is freedom and possibility in this established space. Such a possibility now offers itself not only for that one nature expressing shape, which was the subject of the persuasion, but also offers itself for everything that can show itself in this established space; for everything that is consistent within the opened potentialities. Even this potential does not have to be definitive, the persuading of

---

25 See Plato, *Theaetetus* 191C.

26 Plato, *Timaeus* 49A. František Novotný translates this into Czech as "*chůva*" ("nurse") for the context of other "maternal" denominations of this possibility.

27 Plato, *Timaeus* 47E–48A.

necessity can continue. The potential of phenomena manifesting themselves is "an invisible and formless being which receives all things and in some mysterious way partakes of the intelligible, and is most incomprehensible."[28] And so, *chora* is established, that is, "estate" or "country" or "realm," simply that which is capable of containing something, of placing it. The battle for this potential for containment and placement is, according to Timaeus, continuously played out by some kind of "shaking-up," which searches out possibilities: how to conceive of something new, or how to reconcile present possibilities with the new one, which is struggling to push its way through.

Every individual nature struggles for its own characteristic shape, and this exertion happens in the competition with other natures and with the ties of all relations in the world, that is, in the battle with the necessities of exterior limitations. The exterior limitations are, however, necessary and unchanging only in some aspects and only from a particular perspective and in particular contexts. The battle a nature fights for its place in the world is not then merely pushing with its neighbors for a bit of space, but, far more fundamentally, it is a search for a place in the connections of the world. In fact, in a sense this battle is at least partially the creation of such a personal space in the world—a search for a "niche" through its creation. If we then grasp nature as something existent, its niche (its role in the world) will appear to us only as the way the given entity occurs, as its exterior connections to other entities. The niche of every nature, however, is founded through relationships between natures in the world, whilst the exterior grasp of that same niche is the mirror image of the species determination of a grasped nature, its eidetic and hence shape-related side.

Shapes shape space. It is only in the space we grasp in a certain way and explain as complete that a shape appears to us as occurring in space. The classical philosophers termed shape in connection with matter as *morphe*, which then became the Latin *forma*. As a spatial opportunity, however, shape in Plato is referred to as *eidos*, which is a synonym for the expression *idea*—"insight, appearance, view, shape." Simultaneously though, and not just in Plato, *eidos* is a term for "kind," Latin *species*—both in its logical meaning as a complement to "family" (*genos*), as well as, for instance, in its zoological meaning. Kind is thus understood not only as a method of categorizing natures through their shape,

---

28   Plato, *Timaeus* 51B, trans. Benjamin Jowett, *The Collected Dialogues including Letters* (Princeton: Princeton University Press, 2002), 1178.

but also more deeply through their niche—their type of connections, even in fact as a struggle for certain properties of space, a struggle for prioritizing particular relations in the world. A kind is distinguishable by an insight into its shape (not just the geometrical) and its way of inter-relating, that is, by a disclosure of the references of natural phenomena to thinkable ideality. Thanks to this, at least one side of the world can be known.

Sometimes we can distinguish species determinations by a character-istic shape, to which a nature inclines in its expression. So for example, we recognize a maple tree according to its characteristically palmate leaves, despite the fact that we would struggle to find even two absolutely identical leaves, even on one maple. At other times, we distinguish spe-cies determinations according to the whole habitus, which often relates to the strategy of growth, hence to the method by which a nature leads its battle for being in the world.[29] In this way we can distinguish a maple from a poplar even from a distance—and in fact, we usually differentiate most natures that we can distinguish in a natural way similarly. Only if we had an expert interest would we notice the individual sectional sig-natures of shapes. We can distinguish our friends in a crowd of people through the complete habitus without having to recall clearly each of their individual defining features. It's only when this natural knowledge of their constitution has to be exchanged for an objective description of defining features, as for instance, during a police investigation, that we direct our attention to those signatures retrospectively. But, in a natural relationship we do not proceed like a computer, which, thanks to an extraordinarily complicated program, can identify a scanned picture of a person according to analyzed photographs stored in its memory. For, in a natural relationship with any nature we notice not only the dividing line between it and its surroundings (its exterior shape), but also other features: its interior shape; the way it is constituted; the connection this nature bears to many others; the relation between this nature and our-selves; the way it stands out in our innate experience; its classification into the relations of the world. What we notice is the boundary between that nature and us, which is far from a simply geometrical affair, as it involves the experience of many diverse and reciprocal actions, the experience of the space of mutuality. What we notice is how a certain nature demarcates itself in regard to us as different from us, how the

---

29   See Jiří Sádlo, "O morfogenezi architektury rostlin" ["Of the Morphogenesis of the Archi-tecture of Plants"] in *Geometrie živého* [*Geometry of the Living*] (Prague: Doporučená četba, 1991), 235.

elementality of boundlessness battles for shapes and makes meanings apparent through them.

The space of expression for every nature is made up of all the connections of the world, but the basis of this opportunity is the corporeality of every individual nature. Every nature is, by virtue of its corporeal ("physical," that is, "natural") side, present in the world, it takes part in its connections. The corporeality of every nature is the basis for its space of possibilities and also the basis for its transformations. Every nature is mutable precisely because of its corporeality, as a corporeal entity in the world. The corporeality of living beings is, for them, a component of their life possibilities as well as a kind of memory of their physical being, for it carries the traces of all their battles.

Every nature inclines towards its characteristic shape, yet, at the same time, it actualizes this "ideal" shape only as a kind of suggestion. Moreover, its particular achieved shape is marked in each struggle with its surroundings. A crystal of table salt will always have a cubic structure, but what a specific single crystal will look like is a problem decided by a very large number of circumstances. A maple has palmate leaves and a definite architecture of branches, but the questions of each leaf's appearance, how many leaves there will be, and where each branch will be positioned, are decided during its growth, in the battle for a concrete shape. The shape that every nature inclines towards is "ideal" in that we determine the species of the nature through its identification when we grasp the nature with our consciousness. However, it is also "ideal" in the sense that changes in the shapes of that nature will defer towards it, and do so even without the precise ideal shape being corporeally present in the given nature. This happens despite the fact that all of the details of its approximate actualization have not been pre-decided. Shape then, is something that emerges, through a nature, into a phenomenon and can be distinguished. But it's also that, through which this nature becomes itself and, at the same time, a nature of its kind.

The battle of every nature for its being is thus a competition over something, the definite identity of which is not known beforehand, something that is decided only during the battle. Simultaneously, however, it is a competition that actualizes a "task" or rather, actualizes a field of possibilities. The transformations of every nature fumble around in the space of their possibilities for an opening of new options and in order to optimize the possibilities already laid out. It is a fumbling around for something "that should be" even though the likeness of this "should be" is not decidable beforehand. That will be the temporal dimension of every nature. Time belongs amongst the transformations of a space of potentialities. Whatever enters a world, a field of possibilities and relations, steps into a connection with everything that is in that field; it takes part in the competition for the structure of this same field. It is just by this mutual participation that the field of possibilities is created. Being in the world is a holistic relationship, but this relationship becomes real through the mediation of various meaningful surroundings. The progression of these relations forms the basis of natural time.

The establishment of shapes and the battle for opportunities determine the structure of space. And so the space of natural experience is not simply an empty container without walls and with predetermined straightforward properties (metrics). Space is not just emptiness; it is not only the "nonentity, which is," as the ancient atomists would have it. It was no accident that precisely this too straightforward and artificial conception of space precipitated the collapse of ancient atomism. This is because the nothing between atoms could not prevent their contact, and it follows from antiquity's definition of the atom that with each contact atoms fuse and cannot be divided. What else would differentiate them, if neither their surface nor their volume was distinguishable? Modern atomism escaped from this age-old logical trap with the notion of a field. Space is no longer understood as a mere "nothing," but as a complicatedly structured medium for action, as a complexly formed "something." Likewise, already in medieval atomism, a particle was more of a focal point for a certain structuring of its surrounding space, an epicenter shaping a certain character of the surroundings or, alternatively, the result of the structure of those surroundings.

We can picture species as a tendency towards a particular structure of a field of potentialities. Similarly, we can understand a certain language as a semantic field leaning towards one certain structure. A thing can be understood as an assumed perspective on some area of a field, as an actual interpretation of a field of possibilities. Correspondingly, every word of a language is an actual interpretation of a semantic field, which completes itself through context, that is, the positioning of a word in the flow of speech. The world reveals itself to be a nexus of mutual interpretations and is therefore knowable. Every particular piece of knowledge, however, takes into account only a particular type of relation within the webbing of the world. (Indeed, this metaphor of webbing itself privileges certain ways of interlinking.)

Natural shapes are only very exceptionally describable, without a relatively large effort, using usual traditional geometry. They are so, perhaps, only when it comes to approximations of the shapes of simple crystals. But how do we describe the shape of the seaside, of clouds, tissular structures or bushes? Such natural structures clearly present themselves as structures and hence shapes, but from the perspective of traditional geometrical descriptions they are practically amorphous. Yet even a shapefulness of this sort can be grasped conceptually, as for instance in fractal geometry, which its creator B. Mandelbrot branded as the "morphology of the amorphous." Many such natural structures can be characterized as "self-similar," as a hierarchical structure of similar shapes on various levels of measurement. A simple, and somewhat naïve example can be found looking at a fir tree: a small branch with needles, a large branching branch, and a whole tree, this time with an inverted angle of branching in the lower levels. For over two thousand years thinkers were amazed by the possibility of a geometrical description of many phenomena of the world through simple shapes, and they used this option for the reifying grasp of nature and in the construction of machines. But the fractal geometry of self-similar structures is no "natural geometry" either. It's simply another mathematical apparatus for description. What it allows, however, is the description of natural shapes while committing less violence upon their natures. It is closer to material and corporeal shapes, and it's somehow analogous to the intuition of the medieval "Albertists," who talked of matter as "tending towards a shape," or about matter "pregnant with shape" (*materia inchoata*).

Let us return, however, to our inquiry into the basic experiences of space. Space is an opportunity, a degree of freedom. But it's also an exterior binding condition, since the opportunities concerned are always already structured somehow. The experience of our own corporeality is also an aspect of the experience of space, one that joins the experience of space with the experience of matter, indeed, even with the interior experience of a material nature. Another aspect of the experience of space is distinguishing oneself from other natures, an ability for not only cognitive but also visible distance. Maybe it's because of this that so many of our terms for knowledge are derived from expressions for seeing. Another part of the experience of space is light, thus once again something for the vision, but also for the "luminous metaphors of cognition," as in expressions such as "illuminate, shed light on, in light of, bring to light . . ." The experience of space comprises both opportunities for getting lost, and the potential for orienting oneself.

In the deficient substitution of space using an empty container with no sides, these experiences would also become deficient. Here, light spreads out in a straight line, which is the shortest connecting distance. Orientation is not possible, for no one direction is privileged over another, and wandering around lost harms nothing, for no one place is privileged either. In the space of natural experience it's otherwise, and it's more complicated also in more intelligent imitations of natural space.

Somehow I can always already orient myself in natural space. I always already in some way connect to something in the field of my possibilities; I have always already encountered some obstacles and some limitation. Every limitation of my possibilities is always simultaneously an opportunity, for in struggling against each boundary I gain some shape, I assimilate this boundary into a new layout of my possibilities. Getting lost, that is, losing my bearings, allows me both to return to my more original ("older") possibilities, and to attempt at a new and richer insight into, and filling-in of, spatial structures. Orientation in the natural space of experience is always already orientation in a somehow laid-out space, as, say, in a particular landscape. Getting one's bearings involves connecting to the privileged structures of a landscape, which in the literal sense could be rivers, peaks, or ridges for example. Orientation makes use of those features of a landscape established by its spatial lay-out. Beyond a ridge there will probably be another valley; at the top of a peak a new horizon will open to my view; and following a stream I usually arrive at a river. Orientation in a social space works similarly, as it does in the spaces of other life possibilities.

The ability of every nature to attain a personal shape and hence enter the world as a particular nature competing for its own identity is associated with orientation in the layout of the relations of the world. This is the case even though these very relations can be somewhat transformed through the action of each nature, most often in its surroundings. Orientation is a relation to the world, to the whole horizon of relations and potentialities. It is so even though it's only actualized in a certain "landscape," in a certain layout of structure respecting some horizon and mediated in some neighborhood. For even when we get lost in this landscape, we know at least which way is up, and which way is down. This is a reference to a broader structure of the world, which is more general than a particular landscape, since it belongs to what co-establishes it. In other spaces of our possibilities, the reference to a more fundamental structure of this sort tends to be more demanding and insufficiencies in orientation are harder to redress. The number of fatal wrecks in the field of the possibilities of the meaning of life is usually higher than the number of fatal wrecks in the country. In part, this is because we have, to a great extent, transformed the countryside through civilization in such a way that, at least by our Central European standards, a fatal wreck is only possible in given, wholly extreme circumstances. We are protected from the possible consequences of a loss of bearings by a thick nexus of human residences, paths and their markings, and the various safety bodies of our civilization. In managed landscapes of course, we use these securities usually only for our comfort. For when a country is managed in a way that respects its original natural lay-out, the management merely continues to structure it, offering a sufficiency of opportunities for reliable orientation by itself, at least for people at home in it. We feel ourselves to be at home where we don't have troubles with orientation, where we are incorporated by our surroundings into the complex relations of the world so self-evidently that we need not notice the relations passing outside our immediate narrow horizon at all. Of course, this is something that is built-up in a very complicated, and usually also very long process; something for which culture—that is, artificial growing and constructing—requires a constant sensitive respect regarding more original natural structures and also regarding the broader surroundings. Lacking this, our interventions in the countryside are pure devastation. Blocks of flats, consolidated land, and artificial "forests" or rather fields of trees. As monocultures they impoverish the country not only biologically and aesthetically, but also by disrupting its original structure and failing to provide a sufficiency of new structures. With intrusion like this, the delicate interdependencies of the temporally layered structures of the landscape, including cultural structures, are disturbed, and so we are forced to orient ourselves in such landscapes rather by the help of artificial pointers.

Natural, uncultivated land enables natural orientation. The success of such orientation, however, is very uncertain, and the possible consequences of a loss of bearings could be fatal. Cultured landscapes are broader spaces of home. And devastated land offers predominantly artificial aids to orientation. Such is the approximate layout of the possibilities of humanly managed space on the earth's surface. Of course, the human management of spaces of other possibilities works similarly. And much the same can also be expected in the possibilities of spatial layouts by non-human natures.

The charm of movement in uncultivated country lies precisely in that it reminds us of the structure of the hidden levels of our nature, in that it is an exterior analogy for something within us that is fundamental but hard to manage. In a landscape of this sort, we often have to fight for our relation to the world through our surroundings, sometimes even dangerously, and sometimes without knowing the rules of the battle beforehand, as it is precisely these rules that still need to be fought for. Similar situations arise when new social orders are structured,[30] when new religions are born, when a new area of science is founded, during adolescence . . . The setting up of new spatial structures will always somehow respect the possibilities and bounds of the preceding "natural" ordering of space, but it will also find new possibilities in them. Through the actualization of these possibilities the structure of the web of relations is changed, sometimes to the degree that individual things are interpreted completely differently in the new relations; their nature is grasped (reified) differently. Similar transformations of spatial orientation can be seen also in the morphogenesis of inorganic and especially organic structures—consider, for instance, the justifiable fascination of nineteenth-century science with paleontological and embryological discoveries.

We are always somehow already oriented in the space of the world. But what do we do when our orientation turns out to be insufficient, when from some point of view there is a danger of losing it? Then we turn to the broader structures of the natural world and simultaneously we seek help from the artificial structures created by the culture up until now. Every nature orients and structures itself both with regard to the ever-wealthier connections of relations to the whole, and with the aid of shapes that it has already actualized. When we get lost in open country, we search either for the cardinal points or for signs of civilization. After all, the original meaning of the word "orientation" is the relation *ad orientem*, that is, a finding of the privileged direction where morning light rises after night. Even some basic cultural structures are literally "oriented" in this way, turned to the east, such as altars for example.

Determining the cardinal points means finding the directions privileged only and precisely because of the way a certain section of the country is included through them into the "celestial" contexts of the world. The ancient Greeks would describe this as discovering how *uranos* (heaven) enables the glimpsing of *kosmos*, the ordering of the world. Orientation in space relates to orientation in time, with a connection to the events of the world. Sunrise is one of the sovereign symbols of world events, which simultaneously structures space, establishing a privileged direction. The ascent of light founds the visible space, a space that

---

30   See Heraclitus B44: "The people must fight for the law as for the city wall."

therefore has specific knowable and expressible properties. The ancient and medieval mysticism surrounding light, which on the one hand had a considerable influence on philosophical terminology and many philosophical teachings, and on the other hand, concentrated an interest in optics as a branch of physics, is aware of a conception of space as a structure formed by light, by a kind of ascent of knowability. In the work of Robert Grosseteste, "On Light, or, On the Behavior of Shapes,"[31] for example, the metrics of space are formed through a method of light spreading, and the shaping of shapes is the source of the shine of knowability of individual natures. Space is structured by the knowability offered by shapes; its possibilities and limits are determined by the way this shine arises.

The capacity for orientation is a capacity possessed by observers of the world who can take up important view-points, take note of important places, look in important directions, and glimpse important shapes. Precisely this glimpsing of one direction or shape as important then enables orientated acts, the battle for filling-in shape. In natural experience, in behavior, and during action in the natural world, privileged places, privileged directions, and privileged shapes appear in space, although what is concerned is often a relative and mutable privilege. We see this in embryogenesis, in the structure of thought, and in practical human dealings. Although it's precisely the privileged status of certain places, directions and shapes that enables orientation in space, orientation often weakens the privilege of those fundamental spatial structures. If we want to make use of an understanding of space, then we have to bring that understanding to bear on a different place than just the one where it was glimpsed, and perhaps also in a different direction than the one in which it was first made available to us. An expansion into space would be easier if it happened in an isotropic and isomorphic space. And for this reason, our thinking prioritizes the search for just such freely transferable properties of spatial structures, which can, to a significant extent, be applied elsewhere and at other times than where they originally showed themselves. The effort to think about space as one of the geometrical spaces helps our orientation and also enables effective intervention in the surrounding world. One such attempt to explain all shape in general just from privileged shapes was Euclid's geometry, but

---

31 Robert Grosseteste, *De luce seu inchoatione formarum*, edited by Ludwig Baur (Münster: Aschendorffsche Verlagsbuchhandlung, 1912).

in this process whatever privilege spaces and directions possessed was completely eliminated.

It is possible, with the help of the properties of Euclidean space, to describe perfectly our creations, regardless of whether these are geometrical constructions or material creations: houses; machines. Because the space concerned is purely imagined, and moreover because all of its properties are simply transferable from one place to another regardless of the direction, we can attempt with the help of the properties of this space to describe anything. This makes reasonable sense in all those cases where I describe something pragmatically grasped, which I then deliberately describe not as some nature, but as a definite thing whether it's a nature grasped as an object or my own construct. It's only unproblematic when I grasp a nature in a reifying way to such an extent that I detach it from its interdependencies, when I know that I am doing it and why I am doing it. I could look at the age-rings on a tree stump in this way, for example. However, I can help myself with the properties of imagined space at other times as well, for example when describing a view from a lookout tower, which can also serve as an orientational aid. The extreme instance of the application of space conceived as independent of extra-geometrical contexts is the construction, and subsequent practical use, of a map. We can convince ourselves that the transposition of the space of natural experience onto a geometrically conceived space is not easy, by attempting ourselves to draw a map of a section of country on the basis of having observed it from a number of positions providing views. Natural orientation in a landscape notices privileged places and directions, whereas, on a map, privileged places must be emphasized with agreed signs before they can be seen at all. Conversely, some large landscape structures only stand out conspicuously on a map—and this is perhaps the vindication for constructing a map as a way of trying to gain knowledge about the world.

The degree of difference between the space of natural experience and geometrically conceived space can be demonstrated further by the difference between a cognitive map, which would describe the method of our orientation, and a geometrically constructed map. The cognitive map accentuates frequently used pathways, points of orientation, and other important places, whilst everything else is merely a background, only vaguely sensed, or unclear and without an unambiguous scale for depiction. We might explain to our friend in this way, how, on an outing, we found a little well in a forest that we're familiar with, or how to get to a certain point in a different city by public transport.

Our natural experience, however, also takes perspective into account. It does so both with a purely geometrical perspective and with other types of perspective as well. It's not just mountains and lakes, but also problems, joys, and worries that appear to us smaller from a distance. We could even imagine constructing a map that would, through artificial means, convey more effectively many properties of the natural experience of living space:

In the middle of the map we would mark the place from which we are currently looking. Everything that is within reach of our hands we mark with the scale of six feet to one inch. Everything that is further away, we picture with a logarithmic scale, ideally by the standard of "natural" logarithms—each extra inch from the center enlarging the range of our map approximately 2.72 times. A big piece of paper will fit the whole world. New Zealand will be all around the edge at about 16 inches from the center of the map, whilst reasonably distinct in the middle will be our surroundings. We could make a third dimension of height and depth—and still the whole of it comfortably fits on the table. People will be about an inch high, mountains from seven to eight inches, the moon around nineteen inches above, the sun around 25 inches, stars visible to the naked eye at between 38 and 46 inches, the nearest galaxy at 50 inches, and in fact, even the estimated extent of the universe would still fit under the ceiling. What is important at that moment is in the middle and in the detail; the rest recedes in the background. Of course, such a map has no practical use precisely because it isn't locally transferable. We would have to construct it again in every new place (which we probably actually do in our thinking). Our experience of space is similar to movement. Also of interest is the logarithmic scale, for this relates to the rational quantification of our experience. We encounter it in this sense in Fechner's law of psychophysical perception. Should we want to rationally linearize the scale of the various intensities of our sense perception of a certain phenomenon (light, sound), we would discover the idealized scale to be a logarithmic one, as for example are "decibels," or "star magnitudes" in astronomy. Likewise, many quantities in the real world measured statistically by instruments have a log normal distribution. From the viewpoint of a mathematical description, the connection between the innate and the artificial possesses, suspiciously often, a component describable as a relation between a linear and an exponential scale. After all, it is in similar relations that we formally describe quantitative changes of nature as well: the growth curve, the logistic curve of state change, explosions, and oscillations.

Often in the effort to cultivate land we devastate it. The same is true not just of landscapes but also of every nature, including our own nature and our thinking. In the effort to be at home in the world and to gain knowledge about it, we often also devastate the world. The devastation of space is a considerable portion of each such devastation, and in this, spatial structures are easily distinguishable precisely because they are structures. Many further enquiries can be launched in this direction, important ones for our knowledge of the structures of the world and for apprehending artificial distortions. After all, the entirety of the modern struggle for scientific knowledge and a technical mastery of the world was founded by Descartes's recognition of exteriority, of that, which is *res extensa*, an "extended thing," by the method of *more geometrico*, "the geometrical way." It is an attempt at being at home in the whole world, at cultivating one's own nature. It was also, however, an attempt that veiled the natural world with a web of artificial pointers, one which, fearing the uncertainty of the wilderness of nature, devastated much of our innate experience and much of the outer countryside as well. It was an attempt that tried to grasp the entirety of experience with one unifying insight; one which aimed to convert all the spaces of potentialities of all the surroundings of each nature into shapes filling-in a single and simple space understood in a particular way; one which wanted to declare everything that would not fit into such a description a nonentity, or else to physically bring about that state of nonentity.

7. The structuring of time. Memory. *Horai* (Hors, hours), rhythms and periods. Bearing, sequentiality. Causality and synchronicity. Knowing the past and foreseeing the new. The devastation of time

An encounter with a nature establishes the present. That is, we are present when a nature acts—we can grasp this nature, and somehow by doing so we also grasp ourselves, thus expressing our relation to the world. The world opens up through the present. Through the present, the space of the world opens up as a certain field of possibilities. With every event in this field, a new present is actualized, the field of possibilities mutates. Time is only where there is change, that is, only there, where nature acts. In merely imagined space there is no time, just as there is none in the layout of other solely imagined pure forms. Time does not concern logical operators or numbers. It's only our hands that need some time to sketch these constructions, and our thinking needs some time for their logical contemplation or for adding up a column of numbers. Although geometrical, logical, arithmetical, and other formal relations are capable of interpreting something temporal, and although they need some time for their realization in the world, they themselves are not touched by time. A circle will not age; a number alone will not grow. Time is the structure of the course of events in natural space, the structure of the material course of events. Time belongs among the events of the material structures of space.

Every nature is temporal; it can come to be and pass away. Coming to be always carries with it the stamp of the tendency to passing away.

Everything that comes to be, whether on an inorganic or biological level, also passes away. As already Anaximander put it:[32]

> [T]he source of coming to be for existing things is that into which destruction, too, happens, according to necessity; for they pay penalty and retribution to each other for their injustice according to the assessment of time.[33]

Worldly existence is a loan that must be repaid; it is being in debt. Remarkably, almost all myths and even a large majority of otherwise contradictory philosophical teachings are agreed on this point. The birth of nature is a kind of diversion from "fair" indistinguishability, from equilibrium; it is a separation from boundlessness, and an offence against everything else, an intrusion into the web of relations of the world—one whose consequences it will always be necessary to pay for, ultimately by passing away. Each of these consequences is, of course, a new possibility and a new event; it's remuneration for coming to be, but it's also another new diversion from the indistinguishability of boundlessness. As such, it provokes the cycle again. The space of the natural world is a space of transformations, a space of coming to be and passing away. Every nature that has come to be strives for its development, even at the expense of other natures. But precisely by this inclination towards its own identity, every nature also tends towards passing away; indeed, it is already constantly passing away, thanks partly to the action of other natures. To come to be prefigures heading for destruction. In this, the most fundamental structure of time is determined: namely that this sequence cannot be reversed, that nothing can first pass away and then come to be, despite the facts that coming to be and passing away are never entirely separated from each other and that the inclination to pass away already accompanies coming to be, which is only brought to completion by passing away. This order of coming to be and passing away is the "assessment of time," *chronu taxis* mentioned in the postscript to Anaximander's fragment, which originates, most probably, with Aristotle.

In natural mythopoeic experience, time is the tension for the course of events and establishes the tragic beauty of living the world. The world

---

32   Anaximander B1 (A9), Simplicius, *Physica* 24.13. This oldest fragment, traditionally considered to be philosophical, does, of course, begin and end with an account whose origins lie in an Aristotelean understanding of the pre-Socratics.

33   Translation by Kirk, Raven and Schofield, *The Presocratic Philosophers* (Cambridge, 1983), 117–8.

is a web of mutual grievances and requitals, and only gods and heroes can find and actualize new opportunities in it. Mythic sages try to extricate themselves from the cycle of time; they do not want to provoke the reciprocal grievances of every natural existence, whose tragic beauty the poets narrate. More awoken and independent philosophical thinking unveils the present, differentiates its duration and passing, and occasionally anticipates a brighter future. Metaphysical philosophy and the Christian faith step out of the cyclical time of myths, and look not only to the very beginning of everything primordial, but also and foremost to the present as a gateway to eternity—or even to a future, eschatological or at least enlightened. This more confident position may open itself up to the future, but it's often also tempted to try to outflank time somehow, either with some kind of "entrance into eternity" outside of time, or with the projection of future progress. Meanwhile, however, precisely this consciousness can reveal that the only approach to the permanence of being is the present, that is, every natural encounter—and that the only progress lies in a deepening of consciousness, that is, of the consciousness of the field of one's possibilities in every natural encounter.

We are always much more essentially oriented in time than in space. We have our birth and our past behind us, and our future and our death before us. The present constantly presents itself to us, but only rarely do we actually step up to it as present and not just as we would to the consequences of the past, or as a key to an attempt at controlling future consequences. We can, to a significant degree, move about in space, even at the risk of getting lost, whereas time phrases the events of our lives as if by itself, for it is the presentness of our being. Time is the sign of our material and spatial existence in the world. The most sensitive testimony about our relation to being is how we apprehend time. For this reason, during attempts at apprehending any philosophical teaching, the most important, and yet most difficult question, is precisely the question of how time is understood in this teaching. Thus the whole history of philosophy is, in its most profound dimension, an exposition of the structure of time.

Time is an expression of the integrity of the world. This was registered already in the most famous and most influential determination of time—Aristotle's. Time, for Aristotle, is the measure of motion in regard to what is earlier and later. Aristotle of course, had celestial motion in mind, the movement of the sun across the sky for instance, monitored by the number of degrees moved by the gnomon's shadow on the sundial. These days imagining any approximately uniform movement suffices to "measure out" time. Such a determination of time is, however, mere tautology, for it presumes a determination of "earlier" and "later" and a determination of speed, which is a determination of a number of temporal characteristics. For Aristotle, the measure of time is the movement of the heavens, and everything that we require for its measurement is taken from our spatial orientation, not from temporal determinations. The natural experience of the Aristotelean conception of time still reverberated with peasant farmers who told the time according to the position of the sun in the sky. And the hands of traditional watches artificially model a sundial. Even in Aristotle, however, time is foremost a relationship between potentiality and actualization: the present is actualization. The measure of celestial movements serves only the counting-off of time, the unifying global relating of all changes in the world to the movement of the heavens. Here we have a pattern for an early modern methodical step, that is, for how to achieve, from "celestial mechanics," a model of the physics of earthly courses of events. The reduction of time to the sequentiality of counting is also a feature common to both Aristotle's *Physics* and modern science.[34]

Time was closely studied even in the Latin sphere, which otherwise, down to exceptions, tended to avoid the philosophy of nature. The theology of Latin Christians was marked more by a devaluing of the world rather than with a celebration of Creation. The temporality of everything created is, as regards the eternity of God, understood as trifling. Unfortunately, an enormous influence was exerted by the analysis of time offered by St. Augustine, which unconsciously tied on to the Aristotelean understanding.[35] As with Aristotle, the consciousness of the observer is an integral constituent of time, but, for Augustine, time is only a trifling aspect of the trifling natural world. This is because the past no longer is: it exists only in our recollections, in memory. The future, likewise, is not: it exists only in our expectations. And the present is the trifling divide between these past and future nothings. The limited consciousness of fallen human nature is not able to grasp the eternally existent, and for this reason it grasps apparent, temporal sequentialities. This devastation of the present and of time completes the devastation of all nature and corporeality, which was initiated already in the devastation of matter. True reality is, for thinking that disdains nature, merely

---

34 See Edo Gajdoš, "Přirozená a metrická událost v prostoru a čase" [A Natural and Metrical Event in Space and Time], a doctoral thesis at the Department of Philosophy and the History of Natural Sciences in the Natural Sciences Faculty at the Charles University.

35 Aurelius Augustinus, *Confessiones* 10.7–19.

spiritual and unchanging, outside of time and not natural. Of the intentions of creation and of individual corporeality almost nothing remains.

But what happens to time in a world where we can exactly measure even the imbalances of the Earth's rotation? And a more important question: what is the temporal structure of natural experience? Is it possible to talk of the time of the natural world?

The natural world is a space of transient natures. Every event establishes a present and from a local perspective it's easy to determine the order of individual events. One can place them in a broader framework of coming to be or passing away. But as soon as we try to talk about the simultaneity of diverse events or about the order of more distant events, we stumble on significant difficulties. It's exactly these difficulties that various objectifications of time struggle to eschew, with varying degrees of success. These objectifications take the time of some cosmic event or some mechanical process as the basis for all the temporal structures of the objectivized world. However, in any natural experience that respects the plurality of the natural world something like this is not possible. Every nature has its own time, its own manner of relation between coming to be and passing away, and its own events in which it is present. The synchronicity of the courses of events of various natures is actualized precisely and only in their meeting, which of course does not have to mean their mechanical contact in the same objectivized place, for it happens in any event they have in common. A battle is led for the common world, and similarly for common presence. Even the presence of a single nature is not merely something which just is, but something that is actualized and is experienced in an open encounter. Natural presence points out altered potentialities of coming to be and points towards passing away. Although the world as the horizon of consciousness is also a unifying frame for the diverse temporal structures of individual events, it's still not possible, without force, to infer one commonly applicable time. The flow and its frames, including the aspect of transience, the mutuality of coming to be and passing away, are common, but objectivized time must be introduced by us arbitrarily.

The present—an encounter with the action of nature—is one of the boundary stones between coming to be and passing away; it is an opportunity for relating to the whole, a space for truth to reveal itself. The truth of every nature reveals itself only in its presence, in each of its struggles for shape, in every encounter with it, and in every attempt at its non-destructive grasp. The time frame of every nature, and the truth frame (disclosure) of every nature are one and the same. The attempt of consciousness to widen the domain of common time from several events to a broader whole is analogous to consciousness's attempt to widen of the validity of a truth shared by multiple events. The expansion of consciousness proceeds in this direction, and knowledge struggles for the same goal, but this task cannot be replaced with postulating a single frame for all truth and a single time for all events. All natures point towards unity, both because of their complicated reciprocal relations, and because they have all come to be and they all pass away. But knowledge of this unity comes gradually and conflictingly, and postulates of an overall truth or singular time can either serve this task as auxiliary instruments, or they can disrupt it with the offer of short-cut solutions.

In natural experience, time opens up the experience of identity and alterity. The present opens up access to the duration of that, for which nature, continually flowing between coming to be and passing away, struggles. But time is also the consciousness that none of the intermediate states is the only possible one or even the definitive one. Time is the name for the paradox that we experience identity as a claimed identity within a current of changes of nature—and, also, that we experience alterity only owing to this kind of merely suggested identity. Time is a field of othernesses, of which we are aware only thanks to the struggle for identity.

Associated with this are also the paradoxes of memory. Memory goes with every nature, since every nature carries the traces of its coming to be as well as its battles and past shapes. Human memory is the basis for the identity of personal consciousness. Memory is one of the ways in which what is no longer present is with us. I can easily differentiate the past in memory from the present. Likewise, I can usually distinguish between a recollection of yesterday's event and one from childhood. By this structure, memory offers a foundation for the conscious dimension of time. But it's only with difficulty that I can correctly order more distant recollections into their correct time sequence, and often I help myself with extra-temporal aids (the "logic" of the events) or with the exterior impersonal memory that people artificially create, such as written notes. Among the paradoxes of memory is the fact that I know when I have forgotten something; sometimes I even know what it is that I have forgotten. Indeed, sometimes I can even bring what I have forgotten back to mind. But according to what do I recognize that it is what I wanted to recall, and that I have brought it back correctly when before I had forgotten it? It's from these innate properties of memory that Plato's teachings on anamnesis arose, and similar reflections were made also by St. Augustine.

Caring for memory goes with caring for the meaning of life. This is not merely because many of the contents of memory are practical. Often it is precisely the seemingly ballast contents of memory which prove to be unexpectedly useful. This is because memory is useful not only as a capacity for retaining older layouts of possibilities, but also as a capacity to forget, that is, to naturally sort the meaningfulness of past experiences. Without such classification, orientation in the world would not be possible, albeit that memory usually offers us a different orientation in the world than the one we might wish for at a given moment in view of some immediate end. Presumably it works similarly also with the memories of other natures and natural structures, including the memory of the land.

Every nature stores its ways of relating to the world so far within the structures of its memory. It has here a part of its past at its disposition and can make use of it further. The unremembered past is not available consciously. This is especially important for human nature, because humans relate also to their boundaries, to their coming to be and passing away; they know of them. Humans should also know that they are most limited precisely by what their interests have hitherto absolutely passed by, so much so that even their memory did not ascribe meaning to it.

Every nature enters the present with traces of its changes of shape so far, but it also enters the present as somehow opened-up to future possibilities. Alongside memory, human experience also knows anticipation. We know the dimensions of the past, present and future, and all of this is complicated still further by distinguishing between the progressivity of flowing and the actuality of an event. For natural experience the present is not just that "nothing" between the past that no longer is, and the future that yet is not. It is, rather, the foundation of every experience, a relationship with being. But how can we recognize the same nature in a different encounter—in a different present—as identical, when between times both it and we have changed? After all:

> [According to Heraclitus], one cannot step twice into the same river, [nor can one grasp any mortal substance in a stable condition, but by the intensity and the rapidity of change] it scatters and again gathers. [Or rather, not again nor later but at the same time it forms and dissolves], and approaches and departs.[36]

---

36 Heraclitus B 91 in the context of Plutarch's explanation, *De E apud Delphos* 18.392, cited by Kahn, *Art*, 168.

Every nature—including our own—is different in every encounter (Heraclitus B49A):

Into the same rivers we step and do not step, we are and we are not.

Even (Heraclitus B106 in Plutarch's reading):

. . . the nature of every day is one and the same.

How is it that we can recognize the sun in the morning when it is a new experience of a new sunrise? Evidently of course, because we do so while comparing present experiences with memory. But how is it that such a parallel can be drawn, when what is concerned is never the absolute identity of both? The very possibility belongs among the abilities of our orientation in the world. It is based on a particular way of apprehending the world as a space of a connected course of events, in which acting natures do indeed transform themselves, but do so somehow organically rather than with a leap. We experience ourselves similarly in the task of finding our own identities within a flow of organic and social changes. Recognizing identity is an achievement of consciousness, and the opportunity for it is the battle of every nature for shape. That, which in our experience surmounts the temporal passing of a natural current of transformations is consciousness, i.e., that which opens up the present to us as a relationship with being.

It is not only the individual natures that we encounter which hint at personal identity, but also some experience-related temporal structures. So for example, we talk of the "morning" as of something relatively autonomous in spite of every morning being different, never enabling us to be sure of what tomorrow's will look like. We talk of morning or of evening as if they were individual natures, which we can repeatedly encounter in their diverse transformations and in ours. But what makes morning morning and evening evening? We can distinguish that it is morning by many individual phenomena, that is, according to the expressions of various natures, from that of the sun all the way down to ourselves: it's dawning; we're waking up; it's cool and damp; either the birds are singing or the trams are clattering more than usual; the sun is rising . . . A poet would surely express the special character of morning better than any objectification (regardless of its precision) of any of these phenomena by which we can objectively distinguish morning. And, as long as we are not somewhat mad we distinguish the time in a similar way to poets, whereas it's only in non-natural situations that we temporally orient ourselves according to objectively graspable phenomena. This is because we're dealing more the mutual solidarity of everything that forms a certain period of the day. It is all of this together and only this that constitutes morning, even though some of the individual phenomena can be replaced by others. The experience of morning or of evening, or similarly of spring or autumn, is an experience of a type of temporal epoch, which is a section of a temporal cycle of something important in natural experience. This is the archaic experiential model for an "hour," for what the Greeks called *hora*, which originally signified both an hour (more as in one of the hours rather than a "length" of time), as well as any experiential epoch, whether large or small, often a season in the year. These were considered to be divine beings, the *horai*, the Periods. Heraclitus describes these as (B100):

... the seasons, which bring all things to birth.

The traditional wisdom of the Jews expresses a similar experience thus (Ecclesiastes 3:2–8):

There is a time to be born, and a time to die,
a time to plant, and a time to pluck up that which is planted; ...
a time to weep and a time to laugh, ...
a time to keep and a time to cast away; ...
a time of war, and a time of peace.

The time of natural experience is not like the uniform shifting of a time pointer on a line or half-line. It has a complex structure that shows itself in the "*Horas*," in periods, in epochs that always "bring" something characteristic. Every *Hora* brings something with similar associations each time, but an aspect of this is often something wholly new, as well as the drifting away of something along the prevailing current of being with the flow of time. Every *Hora* is a space for certain events that belong to each other within it; it's a particular fellowship of numerous manifestations of many various natures. It's like an attempt for a certain world in a certain place in a certain period. It's a pronounced horizon of the relations that take part in it. It might only be a short while, or something closer to an "hour" (as "morning" is). Sometimes we can describe it as a yearly season, generation, a cultural epoch of a certain style, and so on. In extreme cases we would talk of it as a geological epoch. Each *Hora* is a segment of some cycle, but these cycles are embedded into each other and sometimes even cross over. *Horas* of diverse orders often have a mutually self-similar structure. *Horas* structure the cyclical level of natural experience. Each refers to a phase of a certain cycle that is also one of the horizons of the layout of possibilities of every nature, one of the horizons of the world. A cycle is the temporal manifestation of the action of differences (antagonisms such as day and night) in their entirety. How do you transform day into night and vice-versa? Just wait!

Individual events succeed each other. Individual *Horas* alternate in their reigns. Cycles close and interpolate themselves into more capacious cycles. Every nature has its own characteristic rhythms and its own fitting timescales. Every layer of the world has its characteristic rhythms. Our ability to experience cyclical rhythms is based on the capacities of consciousness for identifying the identical within the not wholly identical. Rhythm connects to the current from which a structure emerges, one that is grasped through a feat of consciousness and hence extracted from the flowing current. Rhythm is structured in this way, and everything that it brings and carries away can be perceived in a row of interposed periodical cycles. The mythical perception of cyclical time corresponds to this: a distancing from the original, and a return to the original. Likewise with the Neo-Platonic teaching about everything emanating from a unity and returning to a unity. By counting the cycles, we also create a imaginary imitation of the natural flow of temporality, by the help of which we try to relate ourselves to the unity of the objective side of the world. Sometimes we count natural cycles, such as the apparent daily or yearly movement of the sun or geological cycles, at other times we count artificially evoked ones, like the ticking of a pendulum or the oscillations of atoms. Indeed, even our imagined notion of linear objective time is factually based in this way on cyclical phenomena: on a linear conception of numbers that count-off cycles or measure phases of a greater cycle. The linearity of objectively imagined time is, of course, based on the exchangeability of individual counted cycles or oscillations. It stands on a purely quantitative grasp of *Horas*, on an overlooking of the autonomy of each of them. In linearly objectivized time, the concurrence of two phenomena is clearly defined, whereas in natural experience, simultaneity is the result of an encounter in the present, and an aspect of a certain *Hora*. In linearized time, the sequentiality of individual events is perceptibly graspable, whereas in natural experience, sequentiality is obvious only in the vicinity of some *Hora*, some place or some meaning. An experience of succession is always already an experience of a relationship.

Does time have a direction? The unidirectional orientation of temporality's current is already evident just in the irreversibility of many courses of events. Despite its cyclical time structure, this irreversibility of courses of events is surprisingly far more strongly anchored in natural experience than in objective descriptions of the world, which have great difficulty describing the irreversible. As a result, in certain simplifications, one can get the impression that the irreversibility of time is some kind of prejudice of natural experience. After all, natural experience can be captured by a story telling a course of events. The objective reification of nature disregards courses of events and time becomes a mere coordinate for them. Despite this, even the objective description of the world finds its great telling, its metanarrative. This metanarrative tells of the bearing of a world on a certain course. In it, the world is composed of individual things, each one of which has no direction in itself but merely occurs, or at most, battles for its survival and multiplication. The frame of all individual objective descriptions is the story of the holistic course of events, be it the cosmology of the Big Bang, biological evolution, or the vision of social progress or pursuit of knowledge. Objective reification can denature every individual nature; it can denature every horizon of the world and every relation in it, but it cannot denature the character of the world itself—at least not permanently, and not from all perspectives—as long as it doesn't want to simultaneously betray its own standards of approach. The worldliness of the world cannot be permanently or completely abolished, at least not while we remain corporeal living people. It can only be variously interpreted.

But towards what do the courses of events of various natures bear? And towards what does the world bear in its objective description? Every attempt to answer such questions exposes itself to the fundamental danger of overstepping the bounds of natural experience and the rules of objective reification and rational reasoning. Here, every answer opens up the doors to ideology. This does not, of course, imply that the world doesn't bear towards anything. To pretend that we knew this would be ideology as well—only of an especially anti-natural sort.

The relations of concurrence, bearing and sequentiality open up the question of how individual phenomena and events fit together, how they create the world through their temporal relations or rather, how the world asserts itself in their relations. Do the mutually concurrent of these—those that happen simultaneously—belong together more? Or do those with a similar bearing fit together more? Or is it rather that the event belongs with its consequence? Natural experience knows the meaningfulness of all these types of relations, but the objectifying reification of nature primarily grasps only the last of them: the relation between an event and its consequence.

Of course, temporal relations play themselves out within spatial relations, because time is, after all, an event in a space of possibilities. Spatial relations complicate experiences of simultaneity, bearing, and sequentiality enormously, and in particular they complicate the reasoned reified grasp of these experiences. Can simultaneity include events in distant places as well? How would one establish the measure of a maximum "allowed" distance during an encounter?

Spatial proximity is clearly not needed for a shared direction. Nevertheless, we can only distinguish this shared direction once various consequences of events on similar bearings find themselves close together, or alternatively by increasing the measure, by stepping further back. But what does this "close together" actually mean? In what sense are distant events on similar bearings, mutually "distant" at all? They are, after all, close to each other in what is important, the direction of the struggle of nature. They are distanced "only" in objectivized space. We cannot, however, grasp such proximity in reified way, and usually we can't experience it naturally either, not until the point when we suddenly perceive the consequences of these bearings in one visual field, in some encounter.

And how distant can the consequences of some event be in order for us still to be able to experience them and understand them as consequences of that event? They certainly can be distant—that's how consequences tend to work—but how can we distinguish that event in them from a distance and not confuse the consequences for distant echoes of a different event? Can any consequence be exclusively a consequence of one event? And how does the influence of an affecting event span spatial distance? Objectivizing reasoning answers that it's through some movement in space, a movement that, in modernity, it explains as the diffusion of a change in a field. This answer also supplies a relatively straightforward relation expressing the maximum distance at which two things in a particular temporal range can "know" about each other, and hence be related by sequentiality, by action and effect. Sequentiality, however, poses a more interesting problem: is the sequential order of events already a manifestation of their action-and-consequence type of relationship? Seemingly not, at least a reifying interpretation doesn't see it this way. It reads temporal succession only as a prerequisite for assuming a factual and significatory connection. When it grasps a second phenomenon as the consequence of a first, then it will call that second phenomenon an effect and the preceding one a cause. It will then go on to discuss their connection as an aetiological relation, a causal one.

The concept of cause has been through much greater transformations in European thought than we usually care to admit. A "cause" in myth, with Aristotle, Averroës, Descartes and in modern science is something so different in each case that all that remains in common between them is that this type of relationship reaches across time, that it is not a simultaneous relation, and that diachrony is its condition, but not what constitutes it. The relation of causality is established and distinguished by the relation of meaning—and it's precisely for this reason that every further explanation of causality is so dependent on the entire philosophical context. It's only in trivial cases that the meaning of causality is unconflicting and where almost everyone will readily agree to the causal character of the relation of events. One example is the act of striking a match as the cause of a fire being lit. Reifying thinking concentrates on such "close causes" (*causae proximae*) and tries, via their complex concatenation, to search for considerably more interesting "distant" causes. The contexts of these causes, however, are already originally philosophical and often have a character of bearing or intention—a character of finality, which can scarcely be grasped by reifying thought. After all, we sense a significant difference between, for example, the causes of lighting a fire in order to roast a sausage, and the causes behind an arsonist's attack. Both can evidently happen with a match, but we look for motives and aims in entirely different places. Reifying thought attempts to construe this difference purely in terms of the "human factor," whose explanation it then leaves to psychology or another "humanitarian science" whilst presuming to read "nature" without recourse to any of its intentions. The idea of something other than humans doing something intentionally, from an inner movement or for pleasure, is practically inconceivable on the objectified plane. The objectification of every nature removes from it its own temporal structure, its own dimension of truth, and classifies the established likeness of this nature into one frame of imagined time and imagined truth. That's one of the rules of objectivized knowledge, without which this knowledge would not be unambiguous and hence reliable. But these rules cannot be applied to what is natural.

Natural structures of relations involve a richer sequentiality than the mere combination of closest causes. They also include a bearing and simultaneity. This simultaneity, and the intentional bearing revealed within it, may be the most neglected type of relationship between natures. Simultaneity shows itself in the uniqueness of an encounter, and it's precisely due to this singularity that it cannot become an object of science, but can be one of the central themes of philosophical enquiry. A *Hora* is, of course, a peculiar type of a somewhat more global simultaneity, one that, furthermore, has something repeatable in it. An encounter is a kind of local and unique *Hora*. It establishes an openness to the being of the world through presence; it manifests foremost a particular type of world, but does not limit itself to this world *apriori*. A well-understood simultaneity is not determined solely by the common reference of a row of events to the same place in space on an imaginary temporal axis. Instead, it establishes its own view of time. We cannot declare everything that we measure as simultaneous from an exterior perspective to be profoundly simultaneous—just as in advance we cannot consider everything that simply happened later to be a consequence. Simultaneity reveals itself through an understanding of solidarity, as does causality.

Antiquity used the word *symbolon* for solidarity. We still use this word, of course, with several shifted connotations, in the borrowed likeness of "symbol": either as a sign (a chemical or logical symbol), or simply as a synonym for a metaphorical expression (a poetic symbol or a state symbol). Although we could rehabilitate the meaning of metaphor for our thinking and knowledge,[37] what is concerned now is something wholly different. The word *symbolon* or *symballein* originally denotes that, "which happens together," which occurs at once or sequentially as if by accident, but which belongs together through its meaning, becoming understandable only in its mutual connection.

Symbolon is the expression for the experience of accidental events often not being accidental at all, for accidence and causality as mutually relative concepts. It's a name given to the experience that often a thing whose unmediated causes are inane combines connections of meaning that are significant. These connections are, moreover, often polyvalently meaningful—establishing the plurality of their interpretations. A modern analogy for the word *symbolon* is the concept of "synchronicity" as introduced by C. G. Jung and W. Pauli. In everyday terms, it's expressed by Ladislav Klíma's saying that events and geese have one thing in common—they both come in flocks.

---

37 See Jozef Tischner, "Fenomenologia Spotkania," *Analecta cracoviensa* 10 (1978), 73–98.

Synchronicity does not imply that anything compared from an exterior perspective and seen as happening in the same instant necessarily belongs together. Rather, synchronicity means that things that ask to be interpreted together don't have to be sequential and don't even need obvious common unmediated causes, but that they do typically manifest themselves in an encounter. Synchronicity establishes a demand for interpretation; it establishes an understanding of simultaneity and sequentiality; it establishes the polyvalence of meanings and the plurality of truth. Encounters and *Horas* are both synchronistic events. Common bearing can also manifest itself as a synchronistic event. Synchronicity makes possible the comprehension of causality as causality and not as mere sequentiality. It is an expression of mutual analogousness and of the self-similarity of various structures of the natural world; it's an expression of what the ancients called the correlations of the macrocosm. Through these correlations one can glimpse the world's presentness in both its plurality and its temporal current. Objective singular time is a reduction of these relationships, one brought about by making temporal structures geometrical.

Nature reveals itself as present, but it also has its own past and opens itself up to the future. Modern thought attempted to expel history from nature as anthropomorphic, making it a solely human phenomenon. In this conception, knowing nature's past isn't a question of getting a sense of past natural events, but rather an attempt to describe the preceding state of a mechanomorphically experienced world. Here the past is a collection of the causes that induced the contemporary state. We can know it because of our causal apprehension of presentness. The future, likewise, is a mere consequence of the present state of the "world machinery." It can be deduced to the same degree to which we know this present state. The extreme version of this ahistoricality in modern thinking about nature is Laplace's notion of the possibility of a complete and unambiguous knowledge of everything past and future from a perfectly known present. This notion involves not just the question of knowability, but primarily of whether being itself has an unambiguous character at all. Does everything past have just one fixed meaning? Is everything in the future a mere extrapolation of the present, or can the future bring something new as well? It's for this reason that modern thought was so shaken when the idea of evolution became scientific, entering even into the natural sciences.

A battle is fought permanently for the spectrum of meanings of each past effect of each nature, and it's fought not just on the level of our knowledge. Each nature's struggle to enforce tendencies towards its own shape through finding new potentialities is, simultaneously, a reinterpretation of its own past and that of others. This past does not cease to be in new contexts, but is able to pick up different meanings; it can be read differently. Many initially insignificant events or their contexts become significant and vice-versa. Some initially unrelated events join in their meanings; some initially singular significations branch out. Accordingly, the future cannot have the character of something deducible from the present, not because of the weakness of our knowledge or because of the unknowability of the world, but because of the fact that nature and time can always surprise us. Nevertheless, we do sense that not absolutely everything is possible in the future, despite the future's essential openness. It's very unlikely that with the flap of a butterfly's wings everything will suddenly be different. Locally, however, or in certain regions of the world, such cases are possible: as the "butterfly effect" suggests, even an infinitesimal change can decide the behavior of an atmospheric system—a fact that sometimes constrains meteorological forecasts. Indeed, one can imagine, from the very nature of everything existent, that such cases are entirely typical in the world, but that this local life-giving "chaos" tends on the whole to be obscured by some greater and more stable structure, the institution of which is, of course, a ceaseless battle between the many bifurcating areas that constitute it. It's inherent to the world that something more and wholly different to what follows from a particular objectivized projection is always possible in it. But, in the same way, it's inherent to the world that not just anything is possible per se, either in the present or the future. Usually neither geese nor goblins hatch from chicken's eggs.[38] These constraints on the world can be rationalized to a certain extent, enabling amateur predictions, and more so, scientific prognostications. Usually we're able to guess what can be expected. Objective thinking is also often able to considerably specify such an estimate. Only rarely, however, is it able to alert us to the fact that we don't know if the future will bring something new: something completely different.

---

38 This refers to a Czech fable, where a goblin (*plivník*) does indeed hatch from a chicken's egg [translator's note].

8. Evolution—why it tends to be a scandal. Its mechanomorphic reduction. In search of the ontology for which evolution is not scandalous. Bearing into the unknown

Experiencing nature means experiencing change. But if we grasp nature with objective thinking, we reduce its mutability to the spatial movement of a number of parts or particles, which we conceive either as unchanging or as changeable in some other sense of the word, changing into each other for example. The natural world knows movement and change in the strong sense of the word, and knows also the bearing of every nature. The objectively conceived world may be more reliable, but it is meager in its unequivocality, firstly because it reduces movement and change to a change of place occupied in space, and secondly because it has difficulty comprehending a bearing which is open to the future. In classic modern thought, the objectively grasped world is merely the extendedness of matter, organized in space as part of a machine. One cannot expect any directed activity from the objects of such a world, since they are not granted autonomy. Living natures are purged of the autonomic activity of their own bodily dimension. This has been replaced by the combinatorial analysis of compositional parts, something understood, in earlier modernity, simply as a spatial event. There is no place in a world conceived thus for evolution; there's no place in it for a directed change, let alone for a change whose bearing is global. Evolution appears as a dubious relic of natural experience, somewhat colored by the mystical vision of developing nature.

   An evolutionary understanding of nature is precluded by how the majority of basic concepts, by the help of which modern people objectify nature, are grasped: the concept of a species as an ideal or logical entity;

the concept of existence as invariable; the concept of matter as merely inert (*materia inertia*); the concept of space as a passive empty container without walls; the concept of time as a coordinate. Nevertheless, around the middle of the nineteenth century, evolutionary thinking did attempt to establish itself, surprisingly not in mysticism, but in science, in natural science in fact. Natural science, which exercises the modern reduction of nature to occurring objects so successfully, encounters in the domain of the living and in the domain of large time-scales, objectivizable experiences of phenomena whose description at first rebels against this science's scientific ethos. It is an honestly carried-out scientific reduction that discloses the idiosyncrasies of living natures on a macrocosmic scale.

In the nineteenth century, scientific empiricism won through over contemporary scientific conceptual and theoretical apparatuses. It did so, however, only thanks to an essential reduction of this empiricism and its particular explanation—a reduction that made scientific empiricism part of the modern apparatus of mechanomorphic thinking. In 1859 Charles Darwin published his book *The Origin of Species*, expounding evolution by "natural selection." The possibility of something like a species coming to be, changing itself, and passing away was not self-evident, and from a certain perspective it was similar to the notion that something like the number one or the definition of a circle could be subject to development. In this respect Darwin's achievement was understood more as meaning that "species" was a mere agreed-upon taxonomy. However, Darwin's conception of evolution includes not only a change in the properties of living beings (albeit one so fundamental that it changes species determination), but also primarily a change in the orientation of these transformations and the birth of something principally new in their frame. That is the main point which eluded modern mechanicism and which it was necessary to reduce to the state of a mechanism in order for it to be approved by modern thinking as scientific. It's not by accident that numerous textbooks and dictionaries tell us that Darwin "based the theory of the evolution of organisms on a scientific foundation." This is because he explained evolution reductively, namely by "natural selection." This selection is not so much "natural" as it is strictly sociological, mechanistic even. And the denomination of selection as natural is an interpretation not so much of the word "selection," as it is of "natural"—and it is a typically modern interpretation at that. This is why Darwin's theory could be accepted by its time. Selection certainly does belong to the interpretation of the phenomena of evolution. The question, however, is how we interpret selection and its wholly exceptional standing as the driving force for evolution. By selection, Darwin could explain evolution without having to resort to ideas of finality and directed movement. Thanks to this, evolution could become the backbone of natural science.

It would be interesting to track in detail the reactions to the rapid dissemination of Darwin's representations of evolutionary theory, particularly in ecclesiastical circles. In short, this polemic can be summed up as a problem with four layers:

1. The fundamentalist explanation (that is, non-explanation) of the Biblical text and its naïve application to the natural sciences. The Bible's truth is seen as propositionally valid in an objective sense; i.e. in the sense defined by the objectification of truth and its reduction to an unequivocal statement, but which differs from scientific objectification in its hierarchy of the criteria of truth. This conception presumes that we can command truth thanks to its unequivocal written manifestation in the heaven-sent word of God. It's a view that, of course, persists these days in extreme religious wings. More surprising is its presence in Darwin's time in the anti-Darwinist arguments of the traditionally cultural large Churches (such as the Catholic Church, even at the beginning of the twentieth century). In fact, fundamentalism tends to be supported by Aristotelean physics, which rule out essential changes in nature's realm. Why, even in a relatively cultured setting, are fundamentalism and Aristotelean physics invoked in counterargument to Darwin's theory? The likely reason is that type of irrationality characteristic of outraged person's reactions. Such people are incensed not only by their own limitations in being challenged by a new thought, but also by the explanatory limitations of the new thought.

2. The new battleground becomes accidental change and its selection. It's impossible to comprehend an accidental change in the traditional schema inherited from late medieval metaphysics, as it cannot be understood causally. Even natural selection is understood as "blind chance" from this position, as incapable of creating anything qualitatively new. Opponents of Darwin's explanation of evolution derided it on this account as an explanation of an event of the "it happened on its own" kind. A metaphysical understanding of the world cannot show the synchronic character of events, which are, from the viewpoint of objectified causality, accidental. It cannot concede that nature might be active in itself and create the qualitatively new. This is because the metaphysical understanding of the world denatures it by its objectifying grasp. The

metaphysical understanding explains nature in such a way that every change in it demands an extra-natural agent—in the traditional Latin exposition this agent in nature might be "supernatural."

3. However, even Darwin's explanation of evolution (particularly the version widely disseminated in schools) cannot acknowledge the naturalness of nature. The nature of everything natural (or at least living) is, at first, granted by the grand idea of evolution itself, but its explanation denatures it again. The Darwinist explanation squeezes Darwin's discovery into contemporary mechanistic thought. Darwinism thus only changes individual, albeit key, theses of modern thought, and not this thought itself. It's precisely through the influence of ecclesiastical opposition that it shifts towards ever more mechanistic explanations. It emphasizes its reductionism.

4. The main point of controversy of course, is the theme of Darwin's 1871 book, *The Descent of Man*. Darwin's narration of evolution climaxes with the categorization of mankind into nature. This stands in sharp opposition to the tradition of Greek sophistry and the majority of Latin thought, where all that is human is understood as antithetical to the natural. The human is valuable through its culture or through its relation to the "supernatural," whereas the natural is worthless—attaining value only as the object of a human or divine action. Darwin discloses the traditional, neglected theme of Greek philosophy (including the Christian), which, going by the titles of "the place for human-kind in nature," "human nature," or "the origin of human-kind," searches for the place for humans in the structure of the cosmos, precisely through human nature.[39] The unity of the non-living, the living, and the human is revealed through the cosmic relations of all natures. Of course, the anti-Darwinists are not capable of reading this disclosure of Darwin's otherwise than in the caricature of a human derived from a monkey, understood, needless to say, as a machine, and this derivation is, for them, something like a simple copying, as they cannot understand sequentiality in any other way.

With the discovery of evolution, nineteenth-century science rediscovered nature, but it also immediately grasped this discovery in such a way that nature was not recognizable as nature. The explanation of everything human as being from the non-human and living, alongside the explanation of everything living as being from the non-living, was not apprehended as the connectedness of the natures of the various

---

39   See Gregory of Nyssa, *De oppificio hominis.*

dimensions within the horizons of the world, but rather as an attempt at translating everything human into mechanical, chemical, or statistical terms. Darwin's borrowing of the model of a hard capitalist competition from sociology to biology returns in the guise of a self-confirmation through its success in the domain of natural science. Such an understanding of evolutionary theory is typical not just of its irrational opponents, but also for the scientific Neo-Darwinism of the second half of the twentieth century.

A good illustration of how deeply the perception of anything natural has been buried is the attack launched by so called "scientific Creationism" against evolution. The local color for this anti-evolutionary attack comes from its origin in an environment where American fundamentalist sects coexist with a cult of science as the ultimate judge of all truth, that is, from a conflict between uncultured religious fundamentalism and uncultured scientistic fundamentalism. It pitches a monopoly of religious fundamentalism espousing the one truth against the monopoly of scientific fundamentalism espousing all truth, and this deception includes marketing even the former monopoly as "scientific." Whilst Neo-Darwinism in its popularized form pretends that it has no problems with explaining anything whatsoever in the world, and that everything not yet recognized will, in time, be recognized in its conceptual frame, "scientific Creationism" must falsify phenomena and confuse debate by changing contexts without admitting to it. The remarkable side of this is, of course, the missionary success of "scientific Creationism," most of all in the land of science and pragmatism. "Scientific Creationism" ostensibly respects nature. Ostensibly it takes seriously the fact that we see the sun rise and set, that we perceive living nature as living and human nature as human, that foremost it is necessary to interpret these experiences. Indeed, some of its adherents may even honestly intend it in this way. The problematic demand for understanding and interpreting natural experience is, however, replaced with a ready answer. Not only scientific honesty is betrayed, but also religious honesty, and primarily honesty regarding natural experience. This is because the putative "Creation" (*creatio*, creation) is comprehended as a fabrication (*fabricatio*, production). Everything is allegedly accomplished according to a plan and did not appear on its own or by chance. The grasp of nature as a designed product is a yet more reductive grasp than that of science, even if the designer and producer intended is God—a God who is, of course, thus reduced. It is, in fact, an attempt at a complete denaturing of religion without resort to atheism.

Neo-Darwinist evolutionism is provocative in its reductionism, but neither science, nor theology, nor even the majority of philosophy is capable of offering a more open exposition of the world today. The kind of thinking about nature whose level would match the contemporary crisis of nature (the "ecological crisis" of exterior nature as well as our inner nature) remains a problematic and practically irresolvable task. However, it's inherent in the natural order that solutions of problems of this kind can hardly be designed (planned) and then solved. Rather, they solve "themselves" in every act of open perceiving and honest thinking.

Thanks to the discovery of evolution, albeit a discovery reductively grasped, contemporary science is able both to make objectified descriptions of particulars, and to narrate the myth of evolution. It commands a metanarrative that penetrates through individual disciplines and finds places for many particulars in the frame of a great narration, one in which individual pieces of knowledge come to reveal their scientific temperament. When we use the term myth we don't mean something untrue, but something that is a frame for thought. The myth of evolution is the profound truth of nature, albeit a truth that is grasped objectively. Even many renowned scientists are aware of at least the first half of this claim:

> The core of scientific materialism is the evolutionary epic. Let me repeat its minimum claims: that the laws of the physical sciences are consistent with those of the biological and social sciences and can be linked in chains of causal explanation; that life and mind have a physical basis; that the world as we know it has evolved from earlier worlds obedient to the same laws; and that the visible universe today is everywhere subject to these materialist explanations. The epic can be indefinitely strengthened up and down the line, but its most sweeping assertions cannot be proved with finality.

> What I am suggesting, in the end, is that the evolutionary epic is probably the best myth we will ever have. It can be adjusted until it comes as close to truth as the human mind is constructed to judge the truth. And if that is the case, the mythopoeic requirements of the mind must somehow be met by scientific materialism so as to reinvest our superb energies. There are ways of managing such a shift honestly and without dogma.[40]

E. O. Wilson knows about the human myth-making urge; he knows of the profound truth of evolutionary understanding; he knows of its

---

40 E. O. Wilson, *On Human Nature* (Cambridge, MA: Harvard University Press, 1978), 201.

epically mythological character, and he knows of its holistic claim in time and space. However, he understands the natural course of events as following laws, causally chained; he thinks about them merely as reduced to a physical basis. In fact, he even confesses to materialism. He sees human nature socio-biologically, which is as close as we can get to the return of Darwin's methodological loan from the human social sphere into biology. At first, human society was understood as a medium for competition, then ant society as a mechanism, and finally human society again—but now in the same way as the preceding ant society.

The structure of the interpretative concepts, by the help of which Wilson's evolutionary epic is grasped, is an index of the symptoms of the modern paradigm. Should we want to tell a story, then the narration must have a certain structure, particularly if it's to be a true story or the frame of further individual verbally expressible tales. Reducing the sense-structure of the story to abiding by laws, causal chains, physical foundations and so-called materialism, should serve precisely to make the tale reliable. It should mean that its structure can be "indefinitely strengthened up and down the line." It's very difficult to imagine another possible grasp of the evolutionary. Paradigmatic limitation is neither accidental nor willful; it's an expression of our late modern way of relating to nature, an expression of the state of our consciousness, and also an expression of the place in the world's structure where we have positioned ourselves, now in fact with scientific justification. It's a very harsh limitation indeed, one associated with the "denaturing of *physis*." This denaturing of nature is then erroneously assigned to the evolutionary story itself, which doesn't have to be limited by a modern paradigm, and which is quite possibly denatured by such an exposition just as every nature is. However, the only feature that poses a paradigmatic problem here is the method by which the evolutionary story is grasped, whereas its experiential foundation could be thought of as beyond such limitations.

Is it possible to point out an experience of the evolutionary story just in the frame of our natural orientation, that is, in our openness to the relations of the world? The large time scale of the evolutionary story alone, which wholly eludes natural experience, urges circumspection. The evolutionary story was grasped so that it would differ from all other myths by its detailed surveyability, so that it did not have as one of its constituents any golden age or Paradise when the world would have been completely different, inspiring nostalgia. It is precisely this desire for non-difference that disclosed the large temporal and spatial scales established by a certain objectification of time and space. In both tradi-tional ontology and that of modern metaphysics, there was in any case no other chance to reconcile evolution with the habitual conception of existence and reality. The story of evolution is simultaneously a demy-thologization of all other myths. The proffered grasp and interpretation of the evolutionary story makes it into a certain framing explanation of the world, and a way of looking at the world, and hence a world-view. This is probably also what was intended by Wilson's declaration of mate-rialism. However, natural experience of an evolutionary course of events can be a part of the experience of any nature.

The experience of evolution is an experience of the course of events. The course of events goes with every nature, but, as the whole history of metaphysics shows, the course of events is precisely what tries to elude conceptual grasping. The evolutionary course of events is an oriented course of events, an irreversible one. It has its own memory. Although it's able to return to forms similar to those that have already been here, the new forms are already actualized differently and are noted by their dif-ference. The evolutionary course of events always brings something new that also contains within itself the actualization of very old potentialities. Usually it brings something more complicated as well, accumulating not only experiences, but also structures of shape. It's capable of forgetting in order to loosen up to new potentials, but this forgetting does not have to be definitive. A forgotten shape can be recalled in a new context and become the basis for new meanings. Because of all this we often imagine the evolutionary course of events as a gradual unwinding of a written scroll, during which we continuously learn something new. Some of this also casts a new light on the old for us. "Unrolling," or reading, is in fact the original meaning of the Latin word *evolutio*. Of course, the evolutionary course of events does not have a script for what is going to happen next. It is as if the not yet unrolled part of the scroll (or, in our age, the not yet projected part of a film) had never heretofore been un-rolled or written, as if the newly unwound section of the scroll was only now being shaped in its unwinding, even though this shaping is assisted by memory and has many exterior limitations as well.

We promised to attempt an experiential description of the evolu-tionary course of events, yet this last paragraph could easily be read as a description of biological evolution in a time frame transcending natural experience, as a description of evolution as it was disclosed only by a scientific grasp. The last paragraph, however, tried to ex-press the experience its author has with the transformations of his own personal consciousness. And so it is, hopefully, an expression of human nature—albeit more, perhaps, from the perspective of consciousness, which is, of course, inseparable from our relation to every nature. This same paragraph could be read also as a statement about human life experience—or as a description of how time is manifested in our natural experience, that is, as a "description" of time. Time has shown itself to us as our relation to being through the world. Analogies like this probably led Edmund Husserl and Jan Patočka to try to returning to the natural world by exploring pure subjectivity. Let us, however, turn our enquiry away from the subject-object practices favored in modern philosophy, and towards the unwinding scroll and the orientation of the natural course of events.

As long as we want to avoid the misleading impression that even the as-yet-unwound section of the scroll is already unambiguously written, we could, instead of saying "evolution," talk about "expression." It would nicely encompass that searching for an expression (shape) as well as the perspective of interpretation. The problem with this is that we would merely shift the misleading impression elsewhere, that is, into the "core" which would now be merely expressed. Likewise, we could use, instead of the Latin *evolutio*, its synonym *explicatio*, which apart from an unrolling also suggests an expounding. The term *explicatio* was indeed used by the fifteenth-century Latin thinker Mikuláš Kusánský. The world was, for him an *explicatio Dei*, an exposition, or unrolling of God. This implies that there is something in it to be comprehended, but that it is not exhausted by this comprehension, because it is not unambiguously graspable but founds a plurality of possible understandings. Simultaneously the world was for him, a *complicatio Dei* and a *contractio Dei*, that is, some kind of a "shrinking" of unimaginable divinity into many individuals through their individualization, *individuatio* in the material world. It was a particular explanation of the Neo-Platonic description of the relationship between unity and the multiplicity of many individuals, which of course, we don't want to follow any further here. We can't simply end this explanation with the claim that evolution is the self-manifesting action of God, because this would require a demanding theological deconstruction of all the notions connected to it, and a reconstruction of something like, for example, Heraclitus's conception of the relation: One—many.

We find the term "explicate order" also in the work of the physicist David Bohm, where it occurs originally without allusion to Kusánský. It signifies the order of manifested individual phenomena and their evident connections, the order of all that is actualized. Explication is an articulation of sense, similar to when speech articulates its sense in words, and words through syllables. That, which is thus explicated, Bohm calls "implicate." It's not, of course, any "that," or any "something," because a something becomes something definite only in the explicate order. This in itself could lead to the notion that the "implicate order" is some sort of next world: "the beyond," whence something might occasionally surface before sinking back. Or the implicate order could be some kind of area of hidden rule over everything explicate, like a backstage or puppeteer. This, of course, is not how it is. For, every explication transforms the possibility of subsequent explications. It's an event also in the implicate order. It could perhaps also be explained through the implicate view of an event as the perspective of sense and synchronicity, whereas the explicate view of an event is the perspective of significance and the perspective of temporal sequentiality as well as spatial distances. And this is just one among a number of similar variations of the great metaphor for evolution that could be found.

Part of evolution is its direction: the bearing of every course of events, the memory of nature, and time. Every discussion about direction is always already laboring under the suspicion of trying to verbalize, or conversely, trying to obfuscate the end towards which everything bears. Direction itself, however, is not grasped in the reductive grasp of nature—although we do grasp every nature thanks to both its bearing and our own, and, in a certain sense, precisely by that, to which it bears, rather than by what it is.

Nature is transforming; it comes to be and passes away. But in this transformation, this "being half-way," it bears towards its own countenance. When we talked of the "struggle" of every nature for a characteristic shape, it may have given an anthropomorphic impression, as if involving a will. But this "struggle" can often be realized through synchronicity, hence, from an exterior perspective, through "chance"; simply put, through everything that happens. Evolution neither has to be blind, nor driven from somewhere, nor indeed does it have to be pre-programmed. Being steers itself. This is perhaps one of the few sentences upon which scientific "materialism," the ancient thinkers about nature, and mystical theology agree.

Nature fumbles after its shape through many events, after its identity; it develops. It fumbles after something that escapes it, since nature itself is elusive, declining even. It is, however, determined by this fumbling, that is, by that which it actualizes, so to speak, only "half-way," to which it refers, even though it's no fully actualized "something." Nature not only fulfills its species determination by this, but also its own individual identity. Talking of identity and nature is, of course peculiar, because we generally reserve the concept of identity for all that is firm and immobile (thought of as immobile), to which logic and other formal and reliable procedures can then apply. We cannot point out with our fingers the direction in which nature aims, but we can still understand it through experience, and we can also think about it. After all, this is how we recognize natures (and this is also perhaps how the Platonic idea can be understood).[41]

Bearing does not have the character of an occurrence. It's a relation to what isn't actualized. Our consciousness is probably established in this way as well. We differentiate through bearing. Even for Plato, the term *eidos* is synonymous for idea, and the Latin writers correctly translate it as *species*, meaning "appearance" or "insight," but also "kind." Nature's uncertain bearing after its own identity comes from a primordial longing, one the thinkers of late antiquity called *logos spermaticos*. Species determination and individual properties are signified beforehand, but they only realize themselves in the frame of a reaction to the circumstances and events that meet with the nature. *Eidos* can transform itself, but it does so usually more within the bounds of "eidetic variation"—in the bounds of a category of kind. This category of kind itself does not have to be either an age-old generality, nor a merely agreed upon taxonomy with determined boundaries of variation. Kind can be a style of bearing which is able to transform its own paths, so that what could come to pass is that a whole style of bearing transformed itself thanks to the coordination of the events of the other natures in the world.

---

41 See Jan Patočka, *Negativní platonismus* [*Negative Platonism*] (Prague: Čs. Spisovatel, 1990).

9. Living beings—organisms, *metabole*, self-reference; unity in transformation; between chaos and order. The relation to the whole as the openness of the living to the world. A living being as an autonomic whole searching for its own identity in transformation. The secret of sex, mortality and individuality

An encounter with a living being, with anything living, forms the basis of an irreducible natural experience—the experience of nature. Although similar experiences offer themselves in encounters with non-living nature as well—in fact the ancient world does not distinguish between the living and non-living as sharply as we do—we are very often biased towards immediately reducing non-living natures to grasped things, or even objects, to deal with them and indeed already perceive them as such. We lost interest in the non-living when our own products became the exemplary entities. We are, after all, capable of producing even a crystal. And something especially non-living is more amenable to effortless study, preferably it will be unnatural, as is for example a "perfectly rigid body." All else is somehow more complicated and less reliable. It's more difficult to grasp conceptually, and it's more difficult to manage. Everything that is more natural or more living is a source of difficulties, not only for our knowledge via precise concepts, but also somehow in itself, since in its greater complexity and due to its larger wealth of relations, all of its self is threatened more, both by its surroundings and itself; it manifests its temporality more strongly, its having come to be and its transience. Everything living manifests its nativity or growth as well as its transience so strongly that approximations of something living, such as one using rigid bodies, are especially inappropriate. Everything living is a strong manifestation of nature, vividly defying attempts at comparison by mechanical products. So far our investigations have, on the whole, taken nature into account without regard to whether what we are dealing with is living or non-living nature. Despite this, we have pointed out the experience of the natural in a way that preferred the experience of the living. The enquiry could therefore be accused of "phytomorphism" and "zoomorphism," which, like the archaic layers of consciousness, does not sufficiently differentiate between the living and the non-living. However, this is characteristic of natural experience. Whereas, to a certain extent, the reifying grasp pauses before manifestations of life, it does not pause before the non-living, which cannot defend itself from its reification as strikingly or as often and unexpectedly. Grasping a stone is not the same as grasping an animal, let alone a person—despite the fact that on the objectified level, one object is much like another. It's more difficult during an encounter with anything living to disregard the drama of nativity and transience. The living is the exemplum of nature. It surprises us with its own movement; it can jump out of our hands. At other times it might wither in our hands. The analogical manifestation of non-living natures tends to be less dramatic, as long as we're not dealing with something like an explosive.

Everything living grows and ages; it is born, it gives birth, and it dies. And meanwhile, it communicates in a complicated way with the world; it is attendant in a complicated way on the relations of the world. Everything living also has a surprisingly complicated inner structure, which represents a kind of inner world—a physically realized web of inner relations through which it communicates with exterior surroundings. Every living nature is a good example of an entity because it's a bodily expression of caring for oneself and one's relations to the surroundings. The bodily aspect of living nature came, in the eighteenth century, to be termed "organism." The common Greek word *organon* signifies "instrument" or "that, which serves some purpose." An organism serves its own struggle, its own bearing, and its structure is such that this serving is self-similarly distributed on many levels. Hence, we can talk of limbs as of instruments of movement, or of individual inner organs, and again, each of these will act out its own role through certain of its constituent auxiliary inner structures: tissue, cells, and so forth. In attempts at a reified grasp, this almost looks like a purposefully designed complicated ordering on many levels. This ordering is of course "organic," that is, mutually serving its bearing, and not just mechanical. A change of functions in this ordering and variations of its bodily realization are aspects of nature's struggle for shape. In addition, an organism relates to the world through organs, and these then also relate to the world through the whole organism. Organisms have interior and exterior horizons of relations, which shape themselves and transform themselves.

An organism is a whole on a small scale, and this distinguishes it from a mechanism. It is able to repair some breaches of organs and their relations, but dies of the consequences of others. This is something different from when a mechanism breaks down. Some organisms will even renew their entire personal structure from one of their parts. The urge towards being a whole on a small scale is as evident as the urge towards characteristic shapes, and it is enacted through them. The contempt which natural experience holds for parasites may not be based solely on anthropomorphic moralizing about those who "sponge," but might also relate to the fact that these organisms are not self-sufficient wholes. The holistic quality of an autonomic organism needs not have clearly graspable bounds (as bushes do not), but natural experience again privileges those living beings which it sees as visibly whole: trees, animals. Such natures stand out from the background obviously; they can even be counted. When grasping them, consciousness is not perplexed by how to determine a unit for their numbering. They are natures that are significantly pronounced; biologists call them (or rather, called them) "higher" natures.

Every nature is changing. Already pre-Socratic thought associated *physis* with the word *metabole*, "a change, transformation." Nature is always somehow "half-way," what the ancients called "in between (*en meso*)," that is, in a state of its own change, in the process of shaping and retreating. This changing and transforming was known as *metabolismus*. Our reifying grasp concentrates more on the meaning of the word metabolism which links to eating and digestion. This of course, is one of the constituents of the self-transformation of an organism. An organism renews its shapes from newly acquired matter. In an objective grasp, this is for reasons of energy and growth. These viewpoints (especially the energetic one) tend, in living nature, to be frugally optimized. But from other perspectives organisms are wasteful.

The material unity of an organism is always only partial. Its shape and structure change. Organisms belong amongst the natural structures that maintain themselves by the through-flow of energy (dissipative structures), such as, for example, a whirlpool or a flame. But apart from their greater complexity, organisms also express their bearing: they are strongly marked by their own birth and their own mortality; they compete more actively over an idiosyncratic shape and for their own place in the relations of the world.

Whirlpools and flames retain a kind of identity of shape in the flow of new matter and in the flow of energy. Their identity is not based on the identity of matter nor, often, on identity of shape. Rather it's based on the context of the course of events and often also in a certain style of changes of shapes on some scale. It's an identity of process. The same can be said of living natures, but this is still not quite sufficient in regard to natural experience. The appearance of a living being changes with age and with circumstances. Moreover, the temporal orientation of these transformations manifests itself powerfully. Birth is always something more than coming to be, and death always something other than passing away; the identity of a living being is something more than the continuity of a process of changes. From a certain perspective, a living being directs some of its own changes of shape. A living being relates to its surroundings as well as to its shapes, to its bodily structures and its possibilities, and this self-referencing is the foundation for the laying-out of a field of potentialities—the basis for the battle over enacting itself, over its identity.

Identity amidst changes—even changes of shape—cannot be established otherwise than by self-reference. It is an identity that is never fully present, one struggled for approximately as an idea is struggled for. It's comparable to a shape-related and structural course of events, and it is searched for within this course of events. This identity is "cybernetic" in the original sense of the word, that is, in the sense of a mutual alignment of all components and layers of organisms, in the sense of an alignment of the relations between an organism and its surroundings as well as in the sense of an alignment of the relations in the world. This "cybernetic" quality of the struggle of an organism for identity is not fully translatable to mere feedback that is realizable even through mechanical (including electronic), non-living means. This is because everything that lets us realize the actual cybernetic quality of the living is not merely a medium for this realization, but rather a quite literally organic constituent of a living being. It is the living being itself, a result of its cybernetics heretofore.

Self-reference extracts nature from a background of boundlessness. Nature emerges from chaos through its interior horizons and so enters the world of exterior horizons. Living natures do so in a peculiar way, which involves on the one hand a great sensitivity towards tiny stimuli, but on the other hand, a particular area of good stability, secured by self-reference. We know from experience, for instance, that it is easier to hurt living beings than a stone, but also that within certain bounds a living being's wound will heal better than a stone's.

The tentative identity of every self-reference is the dividing line between chaos and a firm order. Every living nature is possible only in the frame of a certain world order, and it also creates a certain order both within itself and in its surroundings. At the same time, however, this order is unceasingly being extracted from chaos, that is, from the flowing of matter and from every transformation. Life is "elemental," but its elementality aims towards a shape, towards an inner order. As long as a living being can move about on this dividing line in such a way that it shapes a sufficiently large space of flexible stability for itself then it is alive. In itself, a fixed order belongs, like chaos, to death and not to life. Algorithms and accidents are extraneous to life. But living nature is able to help itself with something that could be imitated by an algorithm, just as within certain bounds it's able to deal with chance events that cross its path, or even to precipitate such events through its unpredictability. A living being reads chances bodily and synchronistically, it construes them as constituents of the structure of the relations of sense and according to this it responds to them, sometimes as if algorithmically by a "mechanical" reaction, at others through the discovery of a surprising solution in a new field of potentialities.

An organism is a whole and it relates to a certain world as to a whole, although for reasons of material metabolism it relates mostly to its physical surroundings. This is because self-reference itself is, in fact, paradoxically the relation to the world: caring for its own order and its sufficient flexibility; caring for its own shape; fumbling for its own potentialities through those already acted out, and through exterior circumstances. Organisms attempt to read themselves and every exterior stimulus holistically, that is, with regard to their "own" world, with regard to a certain horizon of shapes and events. It's precisely these "higher" living beings, which we perceive in natural experience as more clearly defined against a background and as standing out from boundlessness more distinctly, that usually have not only very complicated inner structures and complicated ways of communicating with their surroundings, but also a more distinct suggestion of something which is, perhaps, the prototype of consciousness. In natural experience they show themselves to be autonomous. Their greater degree of definition is usually paid for at the expense of their regenerative capacities. Yet this enriches the possibilities of their relations to a certain environment. Every definition is a dividing line for communication; it opens itself up to the world and it jeopardizes itself.

Not only do living beings grow, communicate with each other and the world, and die, but they also reproduce. Reproduction is a substantial sign of life. Sometimes reproduction looks more like an extrapolated capacity for regeneration, as for instance during the vegetative multiplication of plants. While on the one hand they dry up or decay, on the other they grow. In this case we have no exact way of determining the individuality of a single member, and all of the properties are also preserved. It is only in sexual reproduction that we come across a specific gamble of life. A whole new organism comes to be, which although inheriting a mixture of the properties of its parents (including those properties that may not have manifested themselves in the parents), does not usually "remember" anything from the individual lives of its parents; the organism is not marked and has to "learn" it again. Modern biology accounts for the necessity of this fresh beginning in sexually reproduced organisms by a phenomenon known as Weismann's barrier. This guarantees that a new individual will actually be a new individual, separate and distinct from its parents, albeit similar to them in most respects. Individuality is chief during sexual reproduction, and it cannot be measured by the degree of similarity or dissimilarity it bears to its parents. We intuitively consider these organisms as "higher," for they share with us humans the specific secrets of the relations of sex, mortality, and individuality. Reproduction is the secret of life, but only sexual reproduction brings with it individuality in the strong sense of the world and death in the strong sense of the word, that is, the death of the individual. The capacity to procreate means the mortality of the individual, and so also the offspring is unique and mortal. Individuality offers itself in the binary relationship between sex and death, which terms, for sexually reproducing beings, are simply different names for life. Individuality, mortality, and sex make sense only in this, their configurational entirety. Incidentally, this used to be the main theme for many consecrating ceremonies, rites of passage, and Eleusinian mysteries. In spite of the rampant thematization of sex in our civilization, this theme remains insufficiently well thought through, for it could be the basis of understanding the relation of human individuality, sexuality and death as well as some individuality also in other vertebrates or perhaps trees and flowers. Sex, moreover, is a powerful source of emotions, i.e., of what, although proverbially not married to reason, is a necessary inspiration and drive for the intellect, which would otherwise be merely machine-like. (On that note, machines are not emotive because they don't have their own bodies and because they don't multiply sexually.)

10. The problem of the knowability of the living. Reducing the living by releasing its soul. The ingraspability of life, which itself grasps. The devastation of life. Life and being

Every attempt at getting to know *physis* grasps something that is reified and by doing so it simultaneously conceals nature. The truth in an individual nature, that is, its disclosure, lies in its manifestation and effect, whereas every grasping, even if it's an attempt at a disclosure, is simultaneously a concealing of nature as natural, a concealing of nature by its reification. However, when it comes to grasped things (grasped either by hand or thought) nature can still act as their depth, at least for as long as we do not wholly isolate the grasped thing from the world, artificially preserving it as such. Our grasp of nature makes life possible for us, it enables our livelihoods and orientation in the world as well as the knowledge of many of its structures. Although grasping veils nature, a skillful grasping will veil nature with something that this nature was bearing towards anyway, something that it strove for. A reifying grasp is thus, apart from anything else, also a fixing of the point aimed at by a certain nature as a thing; it is the active selection of one direction among many for the movement of the nature and of one among many of its relations. It's a selection that privileges and isolates certain relations and directions and then perceives these as definitive and definite from this perspective. The relationship between grasping and manifesting (concealing and disclosing) is not unnatural in any way. It's a component of how individual natures mutually interpret each other in the contexts of the layers of the world close to them. Graspability establishes not just the possibility of livelihood and knowledge, but also sets up a home, an unproblematic region of the world whose everydayness neither betrays nor frightens us, but conceals the life-giving depths.

When grasped, a nature can, to an extent, be domesticated and classified into the context of our surroundings. But it can also, in a sense, be violated, killed or even artificially preserved. Human beings are world beings and not just a beings of their surroundings. For this reason humans can experience the veiling aspect of every grasping, but also attempt to wholly fix some layer of a grasped thing in order to become the masters of their own explanations of the world. Humans can experience the depths and think about the relations of the horizons of the world, but they can also "murder the world" so thoroughly that it will be difficult for them to meet with anything living and natural—at least until this usurped reign does not slip from their controlling hand or consciousness.

Part of our natural sovereignty in the world is our ability to distinguish natures, encounter them, orient ourselves amongst them in relation to the whole, and grasp them. Part of nature on the other hand is its ability to surprise us; it can give us the opportunity to encounter some new dimension of itself, the world and indeed, ourselves. Encountering a newly manifested dimension of a nature can inspire us with awe: it could be a numinous manifestation, opening up a new life opportunity to us, but simultaneously exposing us to some danger. It doesn't just refer to the dimensions of the world that have not heretofore been apparent to us, but also calls our pre-existent notions into question. The numinous is a source of both life and danger. It awakens a sensitivity to beauty, awe as well as fear. It's this kind of natural experience that forms the basis of religious, philosophical, and scientific experience. Each of these domains of human culture, however, deals with the natural bases of its own experience in a different way. The religious transformation of awe leaves itself open to the dangers of self-righteousness; the philosophical transformation to the dangers of ideologization; and the scientific transformation to the dangers of fleeing before nature and technology's aggression towards it. Retreat and aggression both belong to the fundamental ways in which we and other animals relate to various natures and surroundings. However, the objectively grasping form of knowledge is in danger of making flight-or-fight its actual relation to every nature, even in fact, into its relation to the world (the natural world). Both retreat and aggression separate us from unexpected or overly powerful manifestations of nature. Retreat distances us from them; aggression limits or cancels out their effect, either imposing bounds on nature or killing it. Aggression fixes, partially or completely immobilizing nature. As prey to an aggressive grasp that was afraid of an encounter with nature, or at least did not desire such an encounter, nature is already immobile; it's no longer itself, but a mere vestige of what it once was—a vestige of the structures it shaped during its battle for shape in the world.

An aggressive fixing of nature opens up other possibilities apart from retreat before the dynamic quality of nature. Retreat becomes pointless, for aggression also distances us from the power of mutability. Moreover, it brings back game, which is often useful, and at other times a trophy. Truth is hunted on the plains of the world, in the undergrowth and depths of nature (a metaphor found as early as Plato). But this fixing aggression can also separate us from nature as natural if we forget that it is a hunt, that is, a ritual game which is part of being in the world. In this case we would be left with nothing but the useful and useless quarry of our knowledge and the trophies of our skill, trophies symbolizing our new relationship—no longer to the being of the world, but rather to artificial, technical, and institutional products. In losing its orientation, a captured truth stops referring to its own concealment—it's no longer a disclosed reference to the depths, but rather a mere constituent of a plane of consistent sentences or demarcated aims.

Our contemporary experience shows that many of these dangers associated with a scientific approach to everything in the world have come to fruition. Often this is not so much the fault of science itself, as it is that of a scientific approach to everything having been imitated by all those who desire personal and public power without the knowledge and responsibility of those who actually participate in a scientific approach. Science has become a legitimizing myth in modernity, as well as an instrument of power, and imitations of science have supplanted education. Despite this, one can still show, within science, how difficult it is for science to grasp anything that is profoundly natural. We see this in the paradoxes of science concerning living beings and human beings. Scientific methods, which are necessarily and justifiably reductive, hit against their limits in these areas, in encounters with natures whose fixing and reduction strikingly disturb the original motives of enquiry.

Both biology and the humanities gradually adopted the notion of scientificality from physics, which has come to be interpreted in modernity as a mathematical science about occurring entities, that is, about entities which are reduced from all manifestations of nature, especially from life. Can we, however, gain knowledge of the living by disregarding life? Can we know the movement of life through its reduction to mechanical relations? Surprisingly, biology has shown that we can indeed find out a very large amount about living beings in this way, despite the fact that we can only discuss life itself wholly peripherally. Science about the living has also shown that an investigation into mechanical reductions of the living and especially of the dead can offer many revelations, but revelations that conceal natural life. The investigation conceals nature and discloses its own aggression, its fixing. It is exceptional for anything natural and living to be investigated. Dissections are far more common; the liquidized remains of living bodies are analyzed, and often it's enough simply to know something on a model—originally on one that is somehow alive, then on a mathematical one. Is this not, in fact, "necrology" rather than "biology"? In many respects indeed it is, but it tries to be biology. Philosophy cannot offer any advice as to how to achieve this, and even the reference to the paradox about the knowability of the living is not intended disrespectfully towards this science.

The living is organic, self-referential in mutability, and directed in its fumbling. Conceptual knowledge can only either capture something fixed and definite, or it can construct a conceptual imitation of an actual change from something of that sort. The science about the living dismantles the remains of life, mechanically and chemically. It searches for non-living structures in order to explain something living. Fossils or books provide particular examples of easily explored residues of life. Everything that is dead, fossilized or recorded can be investigated as completed and finished; it offers our investigation a fixed shape—at least from a certain perspective. This shape, however, is a relic of something that once lived in the transformations of fields of potentialities. A lot can be found out through such a relic about fields of potential shapes and other life possibilities. However, science about the living is still familiar with, and even sometimes fosters "natural history" in the original sense of the term—as a capacity for observing and apprehending the story of a nature, for expressing the experience of an encounter between thought and living natures and their relations. The investigation of fossils disclosed the evolution of life, but this was instantly fixed within a canonized interpretation. Are not all of the achievements and difficulties of biology one great witness to how, for us, natural life is on the one hand within reach (since we are constituents of it), and on the other how it's always beyond the bounds of every reductive grasp? Is it not also a statement about the strength of life, which still shows itself even through the structures of the residues of the living, in which it is no longer present?

The reductive attempt at grasping life wrestles with life's self-referential character and bearing. Grasping happens through isolating organisms or organs, cells and so forth, from the natural relations of the world and through fixing the world. This is how a holistic perspective of life—what the ancient thinkers called a "soul"—becomes reduced. This is left out in investigations; it's passed over by grasping and released, sometimes also in the sense of being killed. This doesn't happen from a mere will for killing, for mere fragmentation, but from a longing for knowledge. But why is knowledge so aggressive towards life and the soul?

The fact that life and knowledge go together surprisingly badly is a traditional piece of human wisdom. Powers of knowledge do not always support life, and vice versa. Neither studying nor investigating will contribute much to one's health, and conversely, many ambitions for living will clash with study and investigation. Despite this, knowledge still belongs amongst the life desires and necessities of human beings; it is part of human nature. The longing of knowledge for something firm, immutable and not too convoluted is perhaps based in something more profound than just an urge for facile straightforwardness. A possible motive for this longing could be fear of the transience of every nature, including one's own. And a possible motive for reductive cognitive aggression could be a longing for the preservation of one's own soul, albeit at the expense of other natures. Thus, just as we're willing to sacrifice a laboratory mouse on behalf of the sick, so at other times we're willing to sacrifice the nature of any experience on behalf of sure knowledge. It is precisely the tragic beauty of an encounter with a living nature, one holding up a mirror to our being, that can awaken the aggression of reductive knowledge. A rose in bloom will wilt away, but a grasp of its chemical composition points towards supposedly eternal laws. Is not a rose, however, something more than an immobile permanence precisely because of its transience? Isn't it, in fact, a manifestation of the tragic beauty of life with its bearing into the unknown?

The life movement of a living nature was in the past known as a "soul." Soul is the old denomination for self-movement, integrity, self-reference, and having a bearing. It designates the integrity that occurs in relations to one's own bodily shapes as well as to all natures. Soul is the name given to what cannot tolerate the harming of the body or the interior disintegration of its own possibilities. It's a name for the self-referential quality that forms its own shapes with regard to finding its own place in the world, for the bearing that orientates life through its transformations, including the transformation of death. The soul is the movement of life. It's the name for the fact that living nature is an organism and not a mechanism with an implemented program. Soul is the name for the ability of a living nature to read exterior connections and its own interior possibilities, for the search for identity in the midst of mutability. A nature is denatured when its soul is released and living animation fixed. Denatured objects no longer arouse pity in us nor even fear most of the time. In them, the fear of transience is replaced by the oppression of a denaturing, which tries to grasp the sense of a nature's bearing but which is left only with a non-living structure reflecting an instantaneous shape during the nature's denaturing, and a part of its memory.

Soul is the denomination for every capacity for relating, including the ability to grasp. A living nature interprets and grasps and can be interpreted and grasped. However, in some grasps it ceases being alive. We can for instance, fix a rose in such a way that it can no longer even wilt, but this does not make it any more alive. Quite the contrary. Although we try to grasp what life is about, often we do so in such a way that we release the life. This is the case not just in biology, but far more so in theology for instance, or psychology, or in many ways of philosophizing. We try to grasp the eternal, but in our lack of trust in the present, both the eternal and the present elude us, leaving only surrogate eternities, imitations of ideas, definitions, and preserved specimens.

Everything living is a powerful representation of a nature, an exemplum of essence. As soon as we begin to consider anything non-living as somehow more, or more fundamentally an entity than what is living, then we find ourselves in danger of denaturing life, every life, including our own. Denaturing nature is foremost a devastation of life, and it is so equally in the ecological sense and in the sense of life's bearing. Only life itself can overgrow this devastation, for life cannot be pointed out by anything, and even less so grasped. Being itself is not an entity; it cannot be captured.

11. Paradigms—their bounds and transformations. Ancient models—the archetype of the soul. Modernity—the age of the ruling paradigm. Reductionism

We discern nature by grasping it, even if this grasping is merely conceptual. Various different grasps play themselves out in the frame of some style of grasping, which expresses our way of understanding the world, our relation to being. At the same time though, this style of grasping somehow conceals the depth of a nature, its manifesting and hence its non-manifest being. A conceptual grasp tries to obey reason, it longs for a unifying frame for every grasp. This unifying frame is a certain explanation of the world, which, at that given moment, appears to be the only possible one. Concepts, which serve towards demarcating it, appear as ultimate statements about the character of being. They establish a quality of self-evidence with which we then articulate other concepts, and with which the relations between concepts are discussed. Although everything else, that is, everything singular, can then still be refuted or corrected, the fundamental frame enabling a habitual style of giving evidence cannot be called into question, as it is this frame itself that enables us to pose questions in the first place—even though it does so always only for certain questions.

Philosophical discussion, however, doesn't only ask after the inferences of our cognitive propositions and their form. It also, primarily, asks after the presumptions behind their possibilities. It asks after that, thanks to which we can say what we are saying, and it asks why we say it in precisely that way and not otherwise. Philosophical enquiry is able to enquire into the language and discursive mode of our grasping testimonies, and it is also able to enquire into the relation between this discursive mode and the manner of our being in the world. Every conceptual verbalization is an articulation of sense, that is, a way of singling out and linking up our orientation in being, conceivable in a certain type of apprehension of the world.

Our type of apprehension of the world, that is, our conception of actuality, significance, sense and truth, is the frame and the basis of possibilities for each of our grasps and testimonies. To a certain extent it co-determines our perception. The more defined our grasping and articulation becomes, the more justifiable it is for us to enquire into its apparently self-evident presumptions and the simpler it is for us to ascertain the key concepts which structure this frame. Occasionally we can find models of a sort, "most actual" entities so to speak, or at least their type; we find fundamental ideas about the relations of other somehow actual things towards these foundations of actuality; and we find both a level of entity as well as a level of speech considered fundamental or at least privileged. These "exempla" of essence and articulation, along with the structure of the explanation of everything "derived," establish a kind of model order of actuality, which then determines the possible manners of speech we regard as true at that moment. The traditional name given to the model order of actuality is the Greek term *paradeigma*, which in the Latin borrowing is *paradigma*, that is, as long as we do not use the simplifying translation of *exemplum*.

The concept of the *paradigm* became well known through structuralist analyses of the history of science and the language of science.[42] Thomas Kuhn shows how scientific investigation over a certain period appears simply to accumulate pieces of knowledge and to specify its statements by approximation, but how, over a larger period of time, the development of science is characterized more by a transformation in the paradigm of the world within which this science occurs. Some new discoveries do not fit into the paradigm up to that point. In order to be classified into science they require a largely fundamental generalization, one which shows the present state of science to be more like one special case described by the newer one. However, this newer, and seemingly only more general description tends to be possible only at the cost of a change in the conception of actuality, in the conception of truth or knowability. At other times again, a changed spiritual environment will turn the interest of science in a different direction, which at first looks

---

42   Thomas Kuhn, *The Structure of Scientific Revolutions* (Chicago: University of Chicago Press, 1962).

like nothing more than a change in emphasis on areas of interest, but these bring in their wake a change in the style of cognitive process and description, that is, a change of grasp and articulation as well. The term *paradeigma* is, of course, much older—from antiquity. Plato was the first to use it in a sense at least resembling Kuhn's, and he did so with very significant associations. In the *Timaeus* (28D), Plato distinguishes, in his typical way, between "the unchangeable" (ideals) and "that which has come to be" (that is, also that which passes away, that which is experiential) and he asks which of these is the "pattern" (*paradeigma*) for setting up the world. According to Plato, this pattern is made up of ideals, which are eternal and intelligible. The soul also belongs to the structure of the relationship of this model with the world, and it does so in a particularly significant way. It is the middle term between the ideal and what is coming to be, between the intelligible and the experiential, the eternal and the transient, the pattern and the reflection. It is the "world soul," *he tou pantos psyche*, which, through its wholeness, is the pattern of the multiplicity of individuals and in which both the eternal and the temporal are present; hence it is the principle for movement and bearing towards eternal unification.

Further aspects of the paradigm of the world here, are the eternal quality and the intelligibility of that, of which everything manifest in the world is an image (i.e., of ideals). Nature is degraded to "that which came to be"; it is "made" according to a paradigm of intelligible patterns. The soul redeems this melancholy image. The soul is understood as the manner of the relation between the eternal and the temporal—and from this perspective it is, in fact, understood as the genuine paradigm of our experience as well as our own knowledge, for the soul was the paradigm for the divine establishment of the world. The soul is the holistic dimension of all that is singular, as documented even by the tradition of late antiquity:

> They perceive the unity of the soul which is dispersed throughout the whole and is everywhere in itself like the blowing sound through the hollow of a whistle.[43]

The soul establishes, maintains, and renews unity; a whole is an organism and not a mere congeries.

---

43 Tertullian, *De anima* 14, as Heraclitus B67A.

... so does the soul of a human being, when any part of the body is harmed, move swiftly to that place, as if disturbed by the wound of the body, to which it is proportionately linked.[44]

The paradigm of ideals and the world soul is incomplete without the paradigmatic character of the luminous metaphors of knowledge. This parallel, drawn between knowing and seeing, connects to an inclination to the intelligible as the "insightful" and in this insight, to the eternal.

The intelligibility of actual entities is also fundamental for an entirely different ancient paradigm for knowing the world, that is, atomism. The soul, however, in this reductive description, is regarded as one of the occurring entities composed of atoms, and is therefore neither a principle of entirety nor a constitutive component of a paradigm.

The history of philosophy, the history of science and the comparative study of various cultures could afford us many examples of the mutually differing "self-evidences" that structure a grasp of nature and an explanation of the world. However, the true age of the paradigm does not arrive until European modernity, for it is only then and there that one particularly strictly formulated paradigm claims a monopoly over the totality of truth in interpreting the world. European modernity is the epoch of "world-views," that is, different variations of a totalitarian paradigm. Totalitarian here means that they impose one single discursive mode, a single frame for ways of knowing, a single conception of actuality. The paradigm of modern thought is the paradigm of just this style of science, which was founded in the seventeenth century. These days, an educated European usually cannot, without expending great philosophical effort, even begin to imagine that the relation to the world might be set-up differently. For this reason the modern paradigm is usually regarded as "natural," even though "nature" in fact is first grasped only by its prism. The modern crisis of *physis* may well be an outcry precisely on behalf of this ignorance of the paradigmatic character of modern thought and its having been mistaken for a single and self-evident orientation.

Inherent in the modern paradigm is the reduction of the world to one "actual" world, the reduction of the truth (disclosure) of every nature to one "order of objective truth," the reduction of natural speech to unambiguous formal languages enabling unequivocal testimonies—and a row

44　Hisdosus Scholasticus, *Ad Chalcidium In Platon*, Codex Parisinus Latinus 8624, as Heraclitus B67A. Kahn, *Art*, 289.

of further "self-evident" assumptions. Notably, even the majority of officially opposed spiritual currents share this fundamentally paradigmatic structure in modernity. In fact, even modern religious fundamentalists express themselves in this manner, articulating their putative monopoly on truth via these modern structural forms of assumption and testimony. Religious fundamentalism differs from scientistic fundamentalism in the modernity only in its individual "truths" and its greater degree of irrationality in the deduction of these truths.

Paradigms are based on a reductive character of knowledge—one that always accompanies reasoned knowledge. Of course, not every cognitive reduction has to explain qualities by quantities. Anaxagoras, for instance, demonstrated exactly the opposite process long ago. However, the reduction of qualities to quantities offers more opportunities for acting in a purely rational way; it creates space for the formalization of the known, for the use of the formal structures of artificial languages. It's only when these structures replace ideals or even *physis* that devastating reductionism comes into full force, overturning the relation between artificial and natural language. Artificial language, which originated only as an aid for natural language, that is, as one of its newly formed components for the description of certain reductions of nature, is then construed as a direct reflection of essence. Anything not described mathematically or logically is no longer an entity, or it is an entity, but only somehow derivatively, secondarily. Formal, artificial language is directed towards a kind of "basic level" of actuality, which it describes and represents. The "basic quality" of this level lies in the fact that it's a horizon for reductive description. Natural speech is then denied its claim to valid testimonies about actuality, just as nature itself is denied its naturalness.

Of course, many experiences of thought cannot be sufficiently reliably expressed through natural language, and some cannot be articulated through natural language at all. But for these cases, which are so numerous in science, natural language has its newly formed constituents: artificial languages. In encounters with each nature as natural, natural language is the frame for possible artificial languages. In the reductionist destruction of nature, however, the frame for artificial language is a "meta-language," that is in fact, once again an artificial language, one which is yet more distant from the natural, and one which has been formed only for the removal of some few problems of expression. Meta-language has, in late modern thought, replaced the soul—at least as far as a relation to the whole is concerned. It is, however, a different relation, an artificial relation, construed so that the effort for the formal consistency of individual pieces of knowledge did not get into formal difficulties. The illusion of the meta-language resides in the presumption that self-referring structures of speech can be translated without loss into relations between a language and the superior meta-language that gives evidence about it. This, of course, leads to an endless recursion.

Another aspect of the modern paradigm is the fission between "subject" and "object." *Physis* is purged of its subjectivity; it is grasped as an object, that is, as that which my grasping hits upon. An object could be apprehended as the result of a relation to *physis*, but in the paradigmatic cognitive layout it is apprehended as a self-evident occurrence, one that we have registered. The basic level of the description of actuality is then regarded as the one that refers itself to wholly denatured objects, from whose formal combinations it's possible to explain the properties of investigated objects. Subjectivity can then only be human.

A nice example of the paradigmatic disposition of an otherwise profound statement about an important theme can be seen in the earlier quotation from E. O. Wilson. He talks of "scientific materialism," of the unity of the "laws" of the "physical," "biological," and "social" sciences, and of "chains of causal explanation." What does "materialism" mean here? Surprisingly it's not the experience of an encounter with a material nature and the importance of its corporeality in this encounter and in its manifestation in the world. Matter manifests itself to modern thought as quantitatively describable, as "extended" (Descartes: *extensa*), as the basis of the "physical" stratum. "Physical" doesn't refer here to *physis*, but to physics, that is, to the quantitative attempt at a denaturing of matter. Of course, this "physical" level of description is, in the spirit of mechanicism, considered to be fundamental—and it's only in this respect that matter reduced in this way preserves its role as the basis of *physis* even in "materialism" (that is, as an elementary material).

"Chains of causal explanation" cross individual planes of experience and scientific disciplines. They issue from the "basic" level. This could be caricatured with a mechanistic view of culture seeking justification in a mechanistic view of life, and doing so again in a mechanistic view of matter reduced to quantities. Perhaps, however, an echo of the profound experience of *physis* reverberates even in such paradigmatic testimony: in the inseparability of what is human, living, an entity; in the demand of reason for a singular frame for glimpsed relations; and in the experience of the continuity of the natural world in the transformations of its manifestations and descriptions. Of course, a paradigmatic frame needlessly ties this description up with modern metaphysical thinking.

12. Non-hierarchic holistic structure. Everything steers itself through all as if by one wisdom

The modern understanding of *physis* underwent a row of transformations in the eighteenth to the twentieth centuries, which could in some particulars be quite radical. As far as the paradigmatic character of this understanding was concerned, however, they merely revised it. Late modernity also brought with it several discoveries and problems only includable within its paradigm with great difficulty. For this reason many authors either write about a paradigm shift in the twentieth century, or attempt to find a new paradigm themselves. How does this stand in relation to natural experience? Can these investigations also be considered part of the search for a new paradigm that would be more faithful to *physis*? The provisional answer is that faithfulness to *physis* is not compatible with any paradigm, whether it is an "old" one or a "new" one. All the same, *physis* comes to be grasped reasonably through every paradigm, sometimes however, at the cost of such devastations to both *physis* and reason that we humans cannot survive them.

Methods of grasping can be perfected in the frame of every paradigm. It's the paradigm, after all, which emphasizes method. "Perfecting" a paradigm, however, is not possible. This is because to do so, we would have to be in a position where we could see various orders of the world from outside, and moreover, we would have to be able to judge which was "better." Changes of paradigm are changes of the human place in the world, changes of the "voice of being," of ways of manifesting. When it comes to *physis*, there is no pre-arranged best way of describing. Natural experience has no privileged methods of explanation, for every nature is self-referential and at the same time also bound by many relations to other natures, and thus integrated into the world. Although every attempt at untangling these relations into some finite linear likeness is useful for grasping *physis*, it's no longer present afterwards as *physis*. We use all that is grasped, but everything that is not grasped both inspires and imposes demands.

We can at least refer to some of the properties of the structures of anything natural that resist the possibility of paradigmatic description and necessarily elude it. Every nature is a constituent of the world and grows out of its non-manifest dimensions, much as words in natural language are constituents of speech. Nature manifests its shape in the same way that a word refers to its signification. Shape is more of a bearing towards, which happens in complex relations, and signification is likewise only a reference to other significations. Encountering a nature means experiencing a relation between the manifest and the non-manifest. Listening to speech means experiencing a relation between words and language, signification and sense.

Every expression in an artificial formal language is integrated into the context of the language solely by a finite number of precisely defined relations. In this language the meaning of an expression is transferable from one context to another, it is not dependent on context. In an artificial language, "interpretation" is merely a formal substitute for expressions, albeit sometimes quite a complicated substitute. Artificial language enables the production of algorithms, that is, the highlighting of those problems whose solutions do not require consciousness. All of this is indeed advantageous for many tasks, but not for encountering *physis*. Natural speech corresponds to natural experience, which it is aligned to. This alignment cannot be imagined in such a way that certain "correct" expressions of natural speech refer to certain "actual" natures. This alignment works on a far more concealed level. It's based in the mutual analogy of their structures, which cannot be made wholly linear or algorithmic without loss. Natural experience is always convoluted and refers to the unknown. The task of consciousness is to keep vigil, lest this convolution become confusion—and so that areas emerge in the numinous world where it is possible to live in a normal way, where one can be at home, secure, and intimate. Nature has the character of a mutual adjustment. Being steers "itself," but of course this "itself" refers to a sense not translatable into any specific signification.

Nature has no bottom, where our grasping might expect a "basic level," just as it has no "highest entity" above it, which could steer it centrally. Its mutual steering is such that it transforms the manner in which mutual relations are read (interpreted). On any level, it's possible to find a group of manifestations, from the perspective of which one can see that level as the basic one. *Physis* is neither anchored "above" nor "below," but rather it offers orientation, many orientations in fact. Roses will bloom, even if someone finds a hormonal or atomic explanation of why, at least as long as this explanation does not set up fabrications of such a kind that in their wake nothing can flower at all. Each of these explanations, however, contributes to understanding and can indeed be useful. They contribute to an understanding of our cognitive problems, not to encounters with roses.

The wise is one, knowing the plan by which it steers all things through all.[45]

Every forceful grasping of nature is founded on the assumption of some basic level, on the assumption of some chaining-together of causes, thanks to which everything unfolds either from some defined basic level or from defined first causes. Cognitive models like these can be useful locally in a number of cases, but they provide a wholly inadequate substitute for the whole world, which manifests itself during any grasp of any nature by its denaturing.

---

45 Heraclitus B41. Kahn, *Art*, 55.

13. The Philosophy of Living Nature after twelve years. The place for human beings in nature

The chapters up to now represent a new editorial arrangement of a text that came about during the 1990s.[46] At that time, the author was enthused by the possibilities of phenomenology and hermeneutics and had not yet realized how even these very intelligent disciplines shared in the modern paradigm by prioritizing the knowing subject or a certain conception of historicity. How can we think about nature without making ourselves into a source of values, or at least, into comparative judges of the values of everything? Why do we imagine precisely ourselves, human beings, to represent the knowing and willing subject, or even in fact, imagine that this is the basis for our humanity? Would a departure from the self-confidence of the cognitive and willing subject performed in the name of nature not also involve parting with whatever conception of human freedom, of humanism we held up to now, that is, with what we consider as natural to human beings? Would loyalty to nature not bring us back to a mythical conception of fate, even if it can't bring us "back to the trees" in a technological sense? But then, haven't our problems in fact been caused by how long and how desperately we've been trying to distinguish ourselves from animals, particularly from those domesticated by us, to the extent that we now face the further problem of being distinguishable from our own products, from machines?

---

46 Z. Kratochvíl, *Filosofie živé přírody* [*The Philosophy of Living Nature*] (Prague: Herrmann a synové, 1994).

Many would label the succeeding speculations as "naïve realism" or "naïve objectivism." This is because they arise from the conviction that without us the world would, at least in the area around the surface of the planet Earth, look somewhat different, but that nothing else would change. And without me alone, not much would be different in the world at all. The few differences there were might concern me essentially, and a few other people, animals and plants, but the world would probably work in almost exactly the same way as before, as would in fact, the vast majority of human society. On the one hand, it's accurate to say that whatever I do has both perceptible local consequences as well as global consequences and hence affects also the whole world—but on the other, it's equally valid that the number of local consequences is countable and that global consequences represent only infinitesimal corrections, which could only become a kind of juncture for a different course of events under very unusual circumstances. I don't even have to be especially bigheaded to presume that the world would probably change more without me than it would with the death of a mosquito, but as long as I don't sink into an unbridled *hybris*, I won't be able to apprehend this otherwise than as a question of degrees of differences. I won't think that it's only with myself that meaning is given to the world—that it's only my free decision-making on the basis of known possibilities that establishes values.

The question of "values" is perhaps a key one as well as a double-edged one. On the one hand we don't want to surrender this concept because it has a great positive emotive charge attached to it, and moreover it serves us well as a guard against many types of arrogance, such as resisting criminality or political or economic totality. On the other hand, the notion that we ourselves are the yardsticks or even sole creators of values is based in a yet more fundamental arrogance—one that inevitably leads to the assumption of the transferability of values to economic values. Reasonable people will have no intention of renouncing economic values, but at the same time, they suspect that these values can, at least occasionally contradict a kind of intuitive concept of value—one that it's difficult to account for otherwise than through emotions. Although these deliberations are not motivated by the practical problems of ecological activists, we can, nevertheless, borrow a concrete example from this domain: Does a whale have a value? Does it have a non-economic value? In place of the whale we can appoint less living natures, oil wells for instance, or less grand natures, such as a bush in a park. Should we deny all natures their value, then we would either not survive at all, or would survive in a very miserable world, and in a yet more miserable society. Which natures should we then ascribe value to—and what value? If we ascribe it indiscriminately to all of them, and, moreover, if it's some autonomous value not just given by us, then we repudiate the starting point of traditional humanism, that is, our human exclusivity. What then would ensure that the value of every human being, absolutely every one, was greater than, for instance, the value of a sewer rat? And if it isn't, then how will we come to terms with it? Is it enough simply to replace the word "value" as used for what we intuitively understand by its emotive meaning, with the term "the power of nature," both in the sense of individual natures and in the sense of species?

Philosophical investigations of living nature hopefully point out the space for the understanding of a human being's place in nature. Human beings are natural beings, for whom their nature is problematical. This difficulty manifests itself on individual, social, and species levels. Already the myth of Prometheus draws our attention to the insufficiency of human nature's auxiliary equipment (negligible fur, teeth, and claws), which must therefore be augmented with fire, both literally and metaphorically, with intellect. This is natural to human beings as a species.

Society is based not just on exploiting this possibility, but also on a series of driving forces behind egoism and altruism, the relations of love and hate, and the powers of cohesion and contest. This is socially natural, and we meet with many of these aspects also in other social mammals, but it is more complex with us humans, and is so partly because of the reasons mentioned above.

An individual not only competes for his own place in society, without which he couldn't survive, but he is simultaneously a crossroads for both the total insignificance and total exclusivity of each individuality, each singularity. It's natural to human beings that they must be brought-up and educated—and that they then, paradoxically, struggle for their own individuality precisely through this upbringing that so defines them. Sometimes perhaps we long for a definite identity, at others for an oceanic experience of unity with everyone and everything. People forego or, in better cases, hold back and transform many natural desires in the name of society and in the name of individuality. It's during this problematic holding-back of natural relations and reactions that human consciousness arises, and it's capable of grasping all natures because it's that which arose from the world in such a way that it could be included in one unifying frame of a certain being struggling for the entirety of its identity.

A human being is therefore a being with a paradoxical power over its own, otherwise not especially powerful, nature. This applies equally on the level of the species, that is, to every human being, as it does on the social and individual levels, i.e., to various people in various ways. Traditional philosophy explained this by saying that human nature is also the space for the relation of all natures, and that the soul is the "place of all natures." Until the twentieth century, it was appropriate to say that human life is an oriented existence and not a mere objective occurrence.

Asking after nature marginalizes the traditional opposition of nature and culture, as well as the modern opposition of object and subject. It not only brings speech into the foreground, but human corporeality as well. As talking beings we have our own personal experience with the articulation of sense, and we know practically nothing about the extent to which beings of other species share a similar experience. As bodily humans, however, we experience of our own corporeality and inwardness (and also matter, space, and time) naturally. This is an experience we ourselves live, and don't just come to know scientifically.

As long as we regard thought as an attempt to understand any nature, even our own, then every more-or-less thinking human being is, for himself, also an ideal example of nature. This is not necessarily because he's a human being (we don't know this), but rather because he experiences himself from within, because he has an inner experience of his own nature and therefore can, somehow, comprehend also other natures thanks to an analogy with the one which he knows from within. Simply put, he somehow knows what a nature is implicitly, he knows it from himself, from within, even though he must learn everything else, often at the cost of shaking and endangering this foundation. We experience some natures as particularly close to us (usually close people), others conversely as particularly distant, such as minerals, or celestial bodies. Sometimes closeness strikes us as being more pleasant, to the extent that we can't manage without it; at other times, distance seems more pleasant, offering an overview and freedom. We're aware of the fact that life in the world is impossible for us otherwise than at the expense of many natures—such as cabbage for instance, which we eat—but also that this is just how the world works. Of course, every society sets up bounds of sorts around its own being at the expense of other natures, and it does so according to what kind of "stomach" this given society has. In comparison with other possibilities enacted so far, our community has a relatively delicate stomach as far as the literal meaning is concerned, whereas it's almost insatiable when it comes to the practically non-existent limitations on technological and economical plundering.

Already Heraclitus warned us that that our perception of nature is limited chiefly by our consumerist life-styles and plundering (B125A):

> May your wealth (*Plutos*, the Underworld) never fail you, men of Ephesus, so that your wretchedness may be fully exposed.[47]

This is, of course, a pun, albeit a coarse one. Plato also begins his deliberations over the relation between skill and profit with the traditional question of whether a "doctor is a collector of money or a healer of the sick" (*Republic* 1.341–345). Similarly, he goes on to ask whether shepherds aim for monetary gain or for cheese and wool, good sheep and good pastures. They need money as well, but this should be a concern only after all else, that is, as long as the whole system is not to capsize, whilst their main concern should be their pastures and sheep. This is fair enough: Plato was an "idealist," and moreover he considers all of this in the midst of a philosophic framework related to the Good; but how can this attitude succeed in the world of modern thought? Hypocritically, it's straightforward: we simulate altruism. And for this reason populist orators, emphasizing the priority of profit, can often sound refreshingly non-hypocritical. Nevertheless, the ancient hypocrisy did represent a kind of barrier; even simulated virtue has to sacrifice something sometimes, much as does the often useful human rights game. Why not say it out loud that economy and law are a social game, and that life itself is concerned with something different, even if this game will be useful if it has good rules? This, of course, would presume an authority, which the suitability of these rules could be measured against. Moreover, we would have to come to terms with the fact that "morality" showed itself to us in a similarly two-sided position as "value."

After all, "morality" is the traditional denomination for a disincentive from everything our desire might aim towards, but which could be harmful to us or to our human and non-human surroundings. Often we use the word hypocritically, but despite this it acts as a safety-belt like "value" or "right." In a traditional understanding, morality is one of several things that distinguish us humans from animals. If someone were to say that morality is another name for the fear of pleasantness—that is, distrust of nature and fear of its beauty and tragic quality—he would

---

47 Kahn, *Art*, 289, Appendix 1.

in fact be articulating a true statement, but one that is also destructive, undermining the defence mechanisms of our civilization, including a necessary bastion against its own destructive tendencies. He would, of course, have to modify it by saying that morality is also the name for the requirement for a group of many of our desires to be sublimated, for: "it is not better for human beings to get all they want."[48] Can what we uphold emotively with the help of words about morality, be more adequately expressed in a different way? (Let's not forget that historically the concept of a "moral law" attended the birth of the concept of a "natural law." It was understood in such a way that breaking a moral law was immoral, whereas breaking a natural law was impossible. Modern society sets up its own moral laws, albeit often through a very hypocritical account of "human nature" or some "higher law," whereas natural laws are merely disclosed by it.)

Why not talk then rather about responsibility, for oneself and for one's surroundings? To do so, we need not rely absolutely on the double-edged words "value" and "morality." But before whom or before what are we then to be responsible? Before ourselves? That as well, but also before our surroundings and before nature in her entirety. How does this stand in relation to the traditional determination of human freedom? Of course, every determination of human freedom conflicts also with the scientific description of the world (with the scientific world-view), which is, in its very character, deterministic, at least as long as we don't want to resort to the hideaway of quantum phenomena for our explanation of our freedom. Breaking a natural law is, after all, impossible!

It would seem therefore that we have a choice of three options, even if from the perspective of some of them we are not the ones who choose:

1. Mythical fate, with the power of nature and the natural. This conception, however, fits neither our modern ambitions for rational knowledge and freedom of choice, nor the usual conception of responsibility as responsibility for something that is our fault. This would be a world perceived only in a mythic-religious way.

2. The human world of values, rights, and freedoms, along with clearly defined responsibility, but also the denaturing of nature. This would be the world of the sophists. We can also cultivate rational knowledge in this world, as long as we appoint some moral or social authority over it, so that the world is not destroyed.

---

48   Heraclitus B110. Kahn, *Art*, 59.

3. A rational image of the world in which we have a method for everything apart from an instruction for an adequate relation to any nature, including our own. This conception, of course, presumes a certain inconsequentiality preventing us from losing our appetite for clusters of amino acids, or preventing the struggle for the "scientific governance" of the whole of society from succeeding—as that would take away our appetite for anything whatsoever. That would be the world of Cartesian science.

Usually we oscillate between these possibilities and naïvely struggle to join up their parts. But is there yet another option? Is there an option which isn't so jealous of its alternatives? One that would take seriously the experience which says that from certain perspectives (those of the second and third options), our civilization is a unique opportunity, whilst from other perspectives it's entirely decadent? We are, once again, on the subject of fate. We are, in fact, talking of the possibility of a kind of understanding of fate that would be as attentive to nature in her entirety as to our own nature, human nature, including individual nature.

14. Fate, chance and necessity. Necessity as victorious chance. The present as a crossroad of chances and necessity; of determinism and the wholly new. The event of an encounter. Fate as the intertwined quality of stories

For a long time most people have not been able to imagine fate in any other way than as a necessary order, necessary in the deterministic sense of the word. It is difficult to welcome fate understood in this way with pleasure, to say the least. One can regard as deterministic the kind of system in which it is valid that a precise knowledge of all of its parts in one state ensures also the knowledge of all future states (Laplace). Or else: a deterministic system is one in which it is valid that once state B succeeds state A, then state B will always succeed state A (and this can be complicated at will, as for example by introducing a necessary condition C). Strict determinism therefore presumes many things, which have so far manifested themselves to us as very unlikely or impossible: as, for example, the complete separation of a system into its mutually disjoint parts; or the possibility of an unambiguous, completely and unlimitedly precise description of the state of each part, that is, the reciprocal independence of these states from each other so that they can be countable, even in a finite system—all this from the perspective of the philosophy of nature. (From the perspective of modern physics it clashes with the uncertainty principle and some interpretations of quantum mechanics.) Despite this, determinism is in favor, primarily as the unattainable aim of the absolutely reliable functioning of a mechanical machine or stable computer system. After all, what we want a machine to do is the same over and over again, or to react to a precisely defined input in a precisely defined way. Indeed, this is what we produce machines for, whereas every aberration from the deterministic course is, for a machine, primarily a malfunction, one which we can presumably repair and thereby renew the coveted deterministic course. Artificial languages designed for communication with machines or for the communication of defined pieces of knowledge are also constructed so that they describe a deterministic reflection of the course of the world. Along with machines and definitions of pieces of knowledge we thus produce also a deterministic interpretation of fate, one which we don't know how to deal with beyond the scope of life with machines, and which we perceive as a stiflingly ineluctable necessity. The longing for freedom cannot come to terms with it, unless it accepts the determination of freedom as the "appreciation of necessity," or pretends that precisely and only human beings are, unlike all else, constituted in some other manner than a machine, which would, however, be unknowable anyway from the perspective of deterministic unequivocality. If we recall the perspective of nature, then it's evident that the non-machinelike character doesn't belong only to us humans, but rather in fact, to everything except for some human creations.

Still less beloved of people than necessity is chance, except perhaps as an occasional liberation from an unpleasant necessity or as the opportunity of winning something. Chance, however, has no place in a system which is in full working order, at least as long as it's not a chance in the mathematical sense of the word—manageable by combinatorial analysis or statistics, and therefore again a law-bound phenomenon, only this time on a statistical level. We even have a definition for it, for example: We consider a chance phenomenon to be one during which an infinitesimally small change in the original conditions causes a change in the resulting conditions over all hypothetically possible values. So for instance, in the throw of a die, which is designed for this. Some of our machines are capable of producing pure chance: a die, roulette wheel, or a generator of random numbers. In technology we usually want pure determinism, and very occasionally we want pure randomness. In games, of course, we often want both—or rather, a more intricately structured space of possible rational strategies (that is, of one order of necessity, our intention) and of consequences of chance (that is, of a different order of necessity, triggered by a randomly drawn card, throw of the die, or lottery). How does this apply to actuality? Is actuality more necessary or more random—or is it a space of conflicting strategies, chances and necessities, a more fundamental one than our card games? What is the difference between necessity and a chance that has already taken place? And what is the difference between freedom and the fact that something else could have been acted out by chance instead, something other than what happened to happen, and what has manifested itself as necessary ever since? When is a causal description in place, following the order of necessity—and when is it one rather of randomness, whether statistical or stochastic? What is evolution but the fact that the chance that comes to pass and is realized becomes victorious as necessity? Can something ever come to be which is wholly new, something unpredictable from previous states?

A good example of the random encountering of various natures is any crossroad. The traditional image is as follows: Somebody leaves one farm in order to sell a goat at market; another man leaves from another farm having inherited it and sold it, money in hand, on his way to the harbor in order to see the world. The two paths between the first farm and the market and between the second farm and the harbor cross each other. We ask ourselves whether all of the courses of events on both paths are necessary (deterministic) or incidental. In support of the deterministic description is the fact that we can calculate the spatial and temporal circumstances and speeds under which the two will meet, at least as long as we agree that a meeting consists of their passing each other in a defined spatial or temporal range. However, even a description as trivial as this is not without its problems, as it represents only a rational idealization. It presupposes the uniform, or at least the somehow continuously measurable movement of both people. It doesn't make allowances for any willfulness on behalf of the goat; instead it has to deal with them afterwards, and so forth. During a practical enacting this would, because of the synchronization of time, require either an observer in the position of some deistic God (very high up, with perfect vision and distinguishing capabilities) or a very thick web of mutually interlinked observers. Only an idealization to uniform or otherwise regular movement would save us from these problems. But this is a long way from the main point, for such an "encounter," during which the two in fact only pass each other, merely seeing each other and maybe greeting each other, is not a good example of an encounter at all. Nothing happens, and after the crossroad it continues in the same way as before.

The crossroad becomes interesting as soon as we apprehend the encounter as somehow interesting as well, perhaps as an event during which something happens which isn't derivable solely from the pre-existent parameters surrounding the courses of those two people. Let us say that the one with the goat steals the other's money, leaves him lying, lets the goat escape, and goes off to see the world. Or that they become friends on the crossroad, put together the goat and the money, and go somewhere completely different. With a little imagination one can conjure up many more bizarre possibilities, and even these are not absolutely impossible. True, they are somewhat unlikely, but given the enormous number of crossroads, people, and goats in the world, they could, even with a fairly reasonable likelihood, come to pass. However, what concerns us right now is not the degree of probability, but rather the fact that, should an interesting encounter come to pass on the crossroad, then an extrapolation of the description which proved its worth (down to a few "minor" difficulties) before the crossroad, would serve us very poorly for describing what is happening beyond the crossroad. Broadly speaking: we cannot predict almost anything about what will happen beyond the crossroad from what has happened before the crossroad—except for the possibility or impossibility of the encounter itself, both as regards its geometrical and temporal limitations. This, of course, is not to say that the new courses of events beyond the crossroad after an encounter are accidental. One can find descriptions for these as well, which show them on the whole to be law-bound, but we only become interested in this description afterwards. Beforehand we didn't contemplate it at all because to do so we would have to entertain such a very open set of possible descriptions that we wouldn't know very much that was definite anyway, even if we took these concerns into account even then. In plain language: after a battle everyone is a general; after a mishap everyone knows how it should have been done correctly![49]

An encounter, that is, an event, is a crossroad for various descriptions. All of them are rational but they are often of various orders; they are concerned with completely different things. The encounter on the crossroad is a metaphor for an event that changes the context (horizon) for reading a course of events. This is not only a problem for the observer, who, of course, has to change the contexts of his apprehension as well if he wants to understand what is happening; it is inherent in the very character of an event to change the contexts in which certain natures mutually relate to themselves, to the world, and to other natures. Everything is rational; there is no magic being practiced here, rather it is "only" as if by magic that contexts are transformed—heretofore-unanticipated contexts becoming substantial and heretofore-substantial ones becoming marginal. The marginalization of the central and its reverse is not by a long stretch only a postmodern trick. The Greeks would have seen a change of contexts during the event of an encounter as the

---

49 A well-known Czech proverb [translator's note].

domain of Hermes;[50] we can see in it a metaphor for the natural coming to be of something new as genuinely new, which manifests itself as predictable only after it has come to pass. Indeed, it can then form the basis of other new predictions as well.

The event of an encounter is also an example of the course of fate as well as an example of freedom, and it is so without these two being mutually exclusive, without us even having to reduce fate to determinism and freedom to choice between rationally known possibilities. Sophocles understood fate in a similar way, especially in the tragedy *Oedipus Rex*, where he chooses in place of fate the word normally used for chance: *Tyche*. Oedipus proclaims himself to be the "son of *Tyche*" (1080) and the action instantly gains momentum. The plural of this word then signifies the acquisitions of a career, the gifts of fate (1527), which, of course, turn in this case into a total catastrophe.

Objective rationality ties up facts, but events in stories are connected by the telling. Fate can be comprehended as the name for the mutual connectedness of stories. Every event changes the future possibilities of a tale, and every tale influences other tales—the close ones significantly, and the more distant ones very little. However, the issue of which stories are close and which distant can often be answered only in retrospect, and it can change. We know of some crossroads in advance, but not of others. We are wiser afterwards: afterwards we understand, once we know what goes with what.

Freedom can, in this context of understanding, be apprehended as the ability to continue in a story. Likewise with responsibility—not as the responsibility to a certain authority, but to the sense of a story that we do not know in advance. Every nature is distinguished from a product precisely by its not having a predetermined preferred context for its effects and for its exterior and interior relations. It does have its own usual contexts, but equally it's able to surprise through its changes of contexts, sometimes, in fact, it's even able to actively change them itself.

---

50   For more detail on this see Z. Kratochvíl, "Křižovatka" ["Crossroads"] in *Obrana želvy* [*In Defence of the Turtle*] (Prague: Malvern, 2003).

15. Problems of the continuum. The continuity of natural actions and the discreteness of rational objects. Information and its context

Nature's courses of events tend to be continuous. This traditional piece of wisdom doesn't necessarily rule out surprisingly abrupt turnarounds and fundamental changes. It merely states that in retrospect we can always see how such a turnaround was built up to; that even changes like a butterfly emerging from a chrysalis have their own gradual order; that the difference between the as-yet unborn and the born and the difference between the living and dead tends to be of such a character; and that its sharp definition will always to some degree be an issue for our conventions. Even an explosion is a continuous course of events, merely a particularly rapid one that proceeds exponentially in a given phase. A discontinuous change of shape is only possible in rational, linguistic, and virtual reflections of natures. Even the nature of an encounter is continuous, but we cannot describe it wholly rationally and continuously. And should we try to rationalize time, then the present would become so insignificant to us that it would seem like a mere dividing line between the past and the future.

Perhaps what comes closest to the discontinuities characteristic of the progress of our reason is our experience of spatial shapes. Outlines and edges stand out sharply, and only an extreme change of scale or the inclusion of a temporal dimension can make us unsure of when we are before an edge and when beyond it. This is also perhaps the reason why making the world geometrical had and still has such a huge role in rational knowledge. Moreover, the rationalization of space introduced points, that is, something conceived as principally dimensionless. From this alone it's possible to see that what must be concerned are purely virtual entities and merely thought-up ones—by saying which we don't intend to call their import for rational knowledge into question. For something virtual is not the same as something potential, as it cannot be actualized. A point is the simplest example of something wholly fundamental in a virtual world, but which cannot exist otherwise. A point cannot be made actual in reality; it is only possible to imitate the limiting smallness, which is, of course, something entirely different. If the space of the natural world were actually made up of points, then at least the following one of Zeno's paradoxes would have to be valid:

> ... it is impossible for a thing to pass over or severally to come into contact with infinite things (number of places) in a finite time. . . . The passage over the infinite (number of places), then cannot occupy a finite time . . .[51]

The crux of the matter lies in the fact that I can mark out as many points (Zeno's places) as I like, but only exactly as many as I want when I need them for something. Certainly no points obstruct my movement nor my thinking about it in a reasonable, that is, non-Zeno-like way. Despite this we have accustomed ourselves to saying that a "circle is the set of points, which . . . ," simply because this kind of description helps to formalize problems. This "circle" is again a virtual object, one that merely models various round shapes. Of course, a geometer would say that various round shapes are imperfect images of an actual circle. Unless we intend to incite an artificial dispute, we understand what various people mean by what, and why they do so.

Numbers present a greater problem. Nobody would doubt that natural or whole numbers are numbers of something that can be counted, something that can be counted off piece by piece. The expression "five and a half people" is peculiar, unless it's supplied with some explanatory context, an extra-linguistic one for instance. The expression "two and a half buckets" is similarly absurd, as long as it isn't clear from the context that what is under discussion is not the buckets themselves, but two and a half buckets of water, which we need to pour somewhere. Likewise, "half a bread" makes good sense to us because we genuinely want the loaf to be cut, and we're capable of doing it. The expression

---

51 Zeno A25/2 = Aristotle, *Physics* 233A21, from R. P. Hardie and R. K. Gaye's translation in *The Basic Works of Aristotle* (New York: The Modern Library, 2001).

"49 hundredths of bread" is, however, once again, absurd, despite the fact that we understand its rational content well. It is just that normally we would regard it as a still fairly successful semblance of the half loaf and we would only be disquieted if, in place of a half we were given something more like a third. The difference between 1/2 and 49/100 usually only interests mathematicians or lawyers, that is, specialists for various areas of formal thought. The difference is wholly fundamental for rational form, but not for almost anything else. Perhaps for chemists and physicists who work to more precise degrees than to one significant place, but even they are not interested in differences in the twentieth decimal place, whereas a mathematician has to attend to them, since from his perspective two entirely different numbers are concerned. Natural experience uses numbers; indeed, some numerals are components of natural language. Natural experience, however, is interested in numbers of individuals or their order, or "reasonable" fractions, that is, the fractions of small whole numbers. A natural scientist specifies more precisely usual routine dealings with quantities, but a mathematician concerns himself with them formally.

However, even in natural experience we can point out the basis for the mathematical obsession with strict precision—with "attending to the minute." What we have in mind is not the proverbial shopkeeper, but the double role of a number as a quantity and a number as an order. Whether something has 100 instances or 101 instances is often somewhat irrelevant to us, unless what is concerned is something expensive—or we have a kind of sentimental relation to the hundred and first piece. This problem emerges in the situation when what is concerned is not so much the total number, as it is the number of something in a row—odd or even, for instance, if we wanted to divide animals into enclosures. Any grasping relation to nature will accentuate this difference. People, for example, normally pair up with each other somehow naturally. But if somebody tried to do this through a command, like sorting odd and even animals in a row, then they would be fairly attentive to any precedent mixing-up of the order. A similar problem will be familiar to every programmer. For, most of the time it's not very important how many times a loop has run through, as long as the condition for its abandonment is correctly set, and as long as the jump address is correct. But a jump to another address, however slightly distinct, or to a label with a similar name leads to fatally different ends.

Hence, in objectivizing grasps of nature, problems of precision are honed, and in a virtual world they become the main ones. Natural shapes also have a sort of proportional precision of their own (albeit not necessarily always a geometrical one), but the question of precision works differently here. What's important is for the shape to be functional, whether the function is metabolic, mechanical, or distinguishing, signaling. Much can be replaced, caught up, and harmonized; some deviations might even show themselves to be advantageous under different circumstances. The fact, however, that we have exactly two hands, five fingers, and thirty-three vertebrae is a topic for evolutionary history—most probably an important one in some way, since it's so well preserved. The same attachment of an organism to an entirely definite number of hairs would be somewhat absurd.

A remarkable area of the rational grasp of whole numbers is represented by combinatorial analysis and information theory, which rests upon it. The intuitive conception of information apprehends it in a profound dimension in relation to the act of forming, and in its superficial everyday dimension it values information according to its utility, whereas the theory of information concerns strictly disjoint descriptions of the technical representation of arbitrary data. In a description like this, the degree of combinatorial improbability of a given state expressed logarithmically is the measure of information, and this in itself accords well with intuition regarding models. We do have to be aware, however, that in order to articulate this degree we have to know precisely the number of all states which the system can hypothetically attain, namely with equal probability—and that these states have to be obviously mutually disjoint and distinguishable. That, of course, is possible only extremely exceptionally outside the virtual world of combinatorial analysis and without machines produced for the purpose. This is because nature strives for continuity, from which only singular individuals stand out, only some of which we can discern anyway. For this reason alone one can bypass the question of how much information an arbitrary nature carries in advance, with the answer that it carries an incalculable amount—that the accumulation of quantities of information stands in only as a model for the fact that nature is of a different character than data or information. However, data does interest us when it comes to rational knowledge, and the art here is not amassing a mountain of data, but collecting the kind of data we're able somehow to interpret, data which give evidence about the properties of the nature, even when grasped rationally. Apart from this we must keep reminding ourselves that the quantity of information is always related in a certain defined context and therefore that in a different context the quantity of the "same" information will be wholly distinct. (So for example in the character conventions of the program, Word, this book corresponds without pictures to 328 kB, whereas scanning in its pages would take up vastly more, perhaps hundreds of MB; but in order to agree to send precisely this book out of say 256 possible ones on offer, I only need 1 B; and, in fact, to confirm an agreement that it should be printed, I only need a mere 1 b.)

Why are we dedicating ourselves to the concept of information here at all? Because, the cybernetic metaphor has, to a large extent, gradually taken over from the metaphor of mechanics, and this could easily give the impression that what's concerned was something else, something that tries to promise the contexts of an almost Heraclitean *kybernesis*: the mutual steering of the whole. However, the degree to which cybernetics is a science is the degree to which it is yet more strictly formal than mechanics. That is however, with one possible exception that actually does recall the Heraclitean mutual steering but whose full significance is yet to be shown by the future: non-hierarchical webs. The cybernetic metaphor can be useful in many ways during the grasping and modeling of natures, but it is always in fact once again a modeling and representing of nature, and this by means which, in their classic (hierarchic) likeness, are yet more distant from nature itself than the metaphor of a mechanical machine.

16. Between images. Nature and its images. Genres and discourses. The culture of the text and the culture of the image

We encounter various natures in the world and we make various images of them. Sometimes we just imagine them somehow, at other times we paint them or photograph them, and still at others we represent them with complicated techniques, with mathematical models, or specialist or poetic texts. We live flooded by images of multifarious natures, the first of which are already our sense data themselves, which, however, we cannot access otherwise than either through their naïve identification with some nature that causes them, or through one or another of their own rational images. Some images created by us are rational, others fictitious or emotive. To a certain degree we can also combine these types. Some of them are images in a wholly literal sense: photographs, graphics, paintings; others are linguistic and, in extreme cases, textual. In all of these images we maintain a certain order, so that we usually don't mistake what sort of representation a telephone directory is, or what it is of, as opposed to the cases of (for example) a surrealist painting or the notes for an introductory logic course. Our culture distinguishes various genres, which correspond to various modes of representation. As far as linguistic genres are concerned, there are various discursive modes, or discourses, that correspond to them. A cultured person won't search for evidence about the meaning of existence in a telephone directory, nor will he extract archaeological data from the fairy tale of the gingerbread house. Sometimes, however, we can be badly misled, either just because we've determined the discourse of the text wrongly, or because events change the relevant contexts of a reading.

Already Plato laid a strong claim for the priority of forms over their images.[52] There are good reasons supporting the priority of the original before all of its copies—the advantages of the original painting over all of its copies or those of a certain present nature over its photographs or textual descriptions from one or another perspective. So for instance, we can read botanical papers and poems about trees, and we can look at their images, but an encounter with a living tree is more important. The claim for the priority of a form or original is a claim for the priority of natural experience or of an insight into an event—a claim for empiricism. Despite this, we know that the enriching can work both ways: not only can an actual encounter enhance artistic and scientific images of natures, but these images can also enable us to pioneer revelatory encounters (although at other times they can also disable us, for they fix glasses of a certain tint on us). The capacity for employing our own personal education, and not merely being limited by it, is one of the precious features of our nature.

Philosophy is traditionally distinguished from science precisely by not having a prescribed genre for its testimonies. Many celebrated philosophical teachings were written in the most diverse genres, including for example, satiric poetry (Xenophanes), epic poetry (Parmenides), dialogue (Plato), essays (Pascal), or meditations (Descartes). In modern times this situation changes because philosophy lives on in universities and scientific institutes like science itself, most often as one of the so-called humanities. From the perspective of the philosophy of nature this is, of course, not a very happy state for a number of reasons. Not only does it force a more humanistic or logical context on philosophy, but it also makes philosophy feel tied to the preference of academic scientific genres—of which there are not many, and which are all of the same ilk: the scientific text, descendant of the medieval tract and ancient scholarly treatise. It is also understandably difficult to defend a poem submitted as a dissertation. And so, many possible themes and possible perspectives gradually disappear from philosophy's field of vision. Our contemporary culture may be richer in the vibrancy of its images, but its philosophy is correspondingly poorer in this respect. This agrees with the marginalization of philosophy in contemporary society. But the main problem facing philosophical thinking about nature lies elsewhere—in the notion that a certain preferred type of image is, in fact, the original actuality. In this case, we confuse the rational model for the actuality itself, and

---

52 See the allegory of the divided line in *Republic* 6.509–511.

the image appears to us as more actual than the nature, which we then describe as being "driven according to given laws." Maintaining the requirement for a plurality of images, as well as the derivation of each of them from nature, is not then straightforward.

Which of these images of natures are most adequate for the natures themselves? When it comes to questions like this, we already know that the answer will always be dependent on the relations in which one or another nature shows itself to us, or on the motives that drive us to grasp it. But how should one conceive of the relation between each nature and its images? Could it be that nature is somehow "behind" the images, or "under" them—or how? Obviously these are only metaphors, but they are misleading nonetheless. For nature is "that" which is actual, which gives us what to represent in the first place. Nature resides "between" its own images in the sense that it establishes the possibility of their plurality, even requires it. And our human nature is peculiar also because of the zeal and the number of different ways in which it represents, without becoming a representation itself, even though it represents itself as well.

Artistic images have been preserved since prehistory, and we presume there were also images as narrated stories. Textual images from European history have been preserved, amongst which religious, poetic, philosophical and scientific texts played a traditionally large role. It was a culture of text, and we often still encounter it as such, especially in university libraries. Contemporary living culture, however, is ever more pronouncedly a culture of images, not images in the sense of traditional art, but rather of images such as documents, notices, advertisements, games and clips. These cultures are envious of each other like various cultural drugs.

Greek antiquity lived with images and texts. It understood text as a record of speech, almost as a record of sound. But the religious culture of the Jews brought with it a completely different understanding—text became something that preceded both the sound of speech and any natural experience in the Greek sense of the word. Christians, and even more so Muslims, then inherited many of these features. This substantially changes not only one's relation to a sacred text, and then every text, but also the status of language and symbol, including the standing of letters or numbers themselves. These problems belong to the philosophy of nature thanks to the fact that the Greek philosophic tradition was widely reinterpreted precisely from the perspective of text culture, often to the detriment of themes such as nature and the natural. This is not only because the "super-natural" steps into the spotlight, but also because it does so as an explanation of the natural that expounds everything through similar compositional units, like letters in a text culture. A vision presents itself of nature as an open book, as a legible text; it is enough to know the language, and this eventually turns out to be mathematics or the code for DNA. The text of the open book becomes a collection of definitions, equations, codes, and programs. Of course, from the perspective of a text culture it's extremely difficult to understand that we're dealing with images (albeit in these cases they are totally rational representations of certain natures), for a text culture will stake its claim for the priority of text and the fundamental actuality of its symbols. The text culture's approach grasps all available nature in a forcefully denaturing manner and with enormous technical applicability. Indeed, it does so with such an expanded potential for technological applications that it enables the birth of a new culture of images, based more on technical possibilities than the ability of the imagination or the hands. A new type of representing natures is born, one not bound to a concrete objective medium (canvas, paper): the virtual image in a virtual world. But the question remains, is it something other than just a visualization of the fact that our rational textual images of nature were already similarly virtual long ago? Indeed, even the aesthetic style of virtual representation is very close to the aesthetics of that layer of textual culture, which is still showing its worth in the contemporary world.

What happened to our human nature during the virtualization of images? Was it definitively denatured, that is, virtualized, or was it finally emancipated from the hegemony of fixed textual likenesses? As yet we do not know, and it would be wise to defer extreme conclusions. So far, we can only conjecture so much: that what is concerned is not a renewal of the ancient balance between a text culture and an image culture because aesthetics are vastly different, and cultural drugs are changing as well. (Its a pity, there's nothing better than late archaic Naxian sculpture, and older Parthian wine, but people have complained in a similar way for a good few thousand years, and the world hasn't collapsed yet.)

Appendix: Why nature likes to hide[53]

In lamenting the modern denaturing of nature and the parochialism of the world of scientists, we long for our apprehension and experience of the life of *physis* to find an evident manifestation. What a wonderful thing it would be if we managed to construct an experiment displaying the truth of vitalism! Or an alchemical work reproducible under controlled conditions! Or at least a formal logical proof of the fact that actuality is alive and is so through its self-referential spontaneity. How everyone would gape, forced to abandon their denaturings of nature! Somehow, however, this is not viable; and we sense at the same time that our wishful thinking is slightly blasphemous. But why?

Nature is not just her vast superfluity of manifest vibrancy, but also a kind of modest concealment, hiding the springs of both life and being. In the words of Heraclitus, *Physis kryptesthai philei*, "nature likes to hide"; it loves to conceal itself (fragment B123). It is like a healing plant, which grows out into the sunshine, into the visible world, but which conceals its restorative root in the opaque humus (see *Odyssey* 10.302). A sage can succeed in distinguishing such a plant: he separates it thoroughly from others, makes its roots accessible and points it out. He shows the nature of the plant by distinguishing it and letting it work: he can heal through its power, for he is able to make space for its effect. Although the plant loses its life through this, its life was not wasted. It manifested its power, imparted its sense.

---

53 Originally a contribution to the Anthology for the fiftieth birthday of Zdeněk Neubauer (Prague: CTS UK, 1992) 80–83.

How can we know anything living at all? Everything living is constantly changing, "metabolizing" in both the original and contemporary sense of the word: it grows, withers, and evolves itself. Where does the dividing line come for a living being between what it already or still is, and what it already or still isn't? How can we know it on its own as living, and not just as its corpse? In what does a living being differ from a moving or somehow otherwise "functioning" corpse? Is it from the "mechanism" shown in a post-mortem, or by its chemical composition? How does a dead body differ in its relation to life from a broken machine, or a completed chemical reaction? And what connection does this easily investigated remnant of a living bodily being still bear to life, which hides itself from knowledge, to that life which manifests itself so richly before our natural experience?

Plutarch gives the following "biological" explanation of Heraclitus in one of his Pythian writings:

> . . . all mortal nature is in a middle state between becoming and perishing, and presents but an appearance, a faint unstable image, of itself. If you strain the intellect, and wish to grasp this, it is as with water; compress it too much and force it violently into one space as it tries to flow through, and you destroy the enveloping substance; even so when the reason tries to follow out too closely the clear truth about each particular thing in a world of phase and change, it is foiled, and rests either on the becoming of that thing or on its perishing; it cannot apprehend anything which abides or really is. "It is impossible to go into the same river twice," (B91) said Heraclitus; no more can you grasp mortal being twice, so as to hold it. So sharp and so swift its change (*metabole*); it scatters and brings together again, nay not again, no nor afterwards; even while it is being formed it fails, it approaches, and it its gone.[54]

A living being "changes," "metabolizes" in the full semantic range of the word. Through this it is a strong example of a dynamic conception of entity: a river, whirlpool, flame, a living being or human . . . Such is *physis*. It cannot be grasped as *physis*, as it eludes this grasping as a nature; it flees like water from a cupped hand, the more stubbornly we squeeze, the more it escapes. It can only be given an opportunity for manifestation. How is it, though, that it doesn't escape from itself

54 Plutarch, "De Eliot apud delphos" ["The Eliot at Delphi"] § 18. This translation by Sir Thomas Browne, http://penelope.uchicago.edu/misctracts/plutarchE.html in the *Miscellany Tracts* 1683/4.

as well? In the end it does indeed escape and die, but why not immediately? How come a living being doesn't "defecate itself out of substance," doesn't flow through its metabolism sooner that it can age? And how did it come to its "substance" anyway? How did it fill in its own personal shape, which it then succeeds in developing dynamically and maintaining for a certain time? This problem could be traced from the pre-Socratics to the theoreticians of morphogenetic fields.

A dynamic conception of entity does not relate to something that just flows, but rather, to something that transforms itself spontaneously in such a way that precisely through this spontaneity of change it refers itself to itself. The examples of the whirlpool and the flame are illustrative: matter changes, perhaps even from the core, but the delicate continuity of these entities lies in their characteristic changes of shape. Shape changes as well, but these changes create a self-referential order, which, in these simple examples, is sometimes even reducible to mere feedback. Their identity is dynamic, and this is where their "life" as elements resides. The explanation through feedback is our reductive grasp of their tendency to self-identity. It is far more complex with living beings—and the difference between their vital character (nature) and our grasping explanations is far greater. We have the same experience with our own consciousness: it reacts to new stimuli, it is constantly threatened both by chaos and paralysis, and we can even model some of its manifestations with logic or cybernetics. The struggle for human self-identity within the changes of human life is another great example of life with its *metabole* and its self-referentiality, what the ancients used to call the "soul." The soul is a holistic view of a living being; it is the relation a living being bears to itself as a whole, as well as the openness of a living being to the world. Precisely this identity of openness and self-reference belongs to the secrets of life; it is part of searching for one's own measures, or searching for a personal and species identity. Our consciousness manifests itself in speech. This also has its own transformations and searches for identity. It laboriously articulates syllables and words in relation to the whole of the sentence and to the whole of the speech. It is permanently in danger of decomposition or paralysis, but while it lives, it faces up to these with spontaneity employed in self-reference. Linguistic puns are more significant for the life of speech than the formal reflections made on its development.

Nature emerges from chaos through her self-referentiality, through what the ancients called "the logos of the soul" (Heraclitus B45). *Logos* is an interpretable expression, an opportunity for interpretation, hence, it "makes sense," "accords with reason," and does so through shape and structure. The *logos* of a conscious soul—speech—classifies the shapes (*logoi*, meanings, species) of individual natures into the whole of some kind of understanding of the world and of oneself. By this, speech somehow grasps every nature, but always precisely only somehow. It grasps nature by some of the vanishing points of her bearing, by some "idea" to which that nature is bearing, that is, by the one that somehow corresponds to my own contemporary search for my own shape and its apprehension. In Europe, it's customary to call natures grasped in this way "things." Speech can then also be pragmatic, if it wants. But it doesn't have to be, if it doesn't want to. This is what distinguishes the speech of poets from the speech of scientists—a poet says: "Things can be anything, but you have to tell them first" (Rilke, of a children's game). Poetic language knows that nature can be grasped in various ways, although not arbitrarily, or, more precisely, not willfully. It is necessary to listen to nature and to help her manifest her vivid offers of meanings. But pragmatic language, particularly conceptual language, often stoops to the illusion that it "caught the cat in the only possible and correct way, and that the cat is still alive."

Conceptual language, and especially the formalized language of science or certain styles of philosophy, erects a safety barrier against our willfulness differently than does poetic speech. In the frame of a formalized language, one can do nothing other than formally deduce or construe. Anything else would break the rules of the game. The way in which language is formalized, or the way in which concepts are adopted into a language, is, in this level's frame, an obligatory medium for accessing truth. That is, the truth which appeared as unambiguous, the truth about an entity which "is"; the truth, which came to light on the basis (foundation) of a certain paradigm, i.e., on the basis of a certain conception of some "firm" character of entity.

The rediscovery of a lost sense for *physis* is possible only when fundamentalism falls, and when the bottomless depth of the levels of truth is revealed. *Physis* has its source somewhere down there, not on the "bottom," but rather simply in "there" as a reference. It rises from a gaping chasm (from "chaos") and not from a defined level of description. It longs for one of those structures that will occur to it, and which it will succeed in enacting to a certain extent. It doesn't long for a contradiction-free description. We always grasp *physis* on some level, and this level is a level precisely because of its inner consistency. We try for the deepest possible grasping, but we know that every disclosure is finite, and this guards us against the temptation to declare a new level of our thinking experience to be the new, unique, and correct foundation.

Consciousness illuminates the depths when it assimilates their manifestations. That is part of the road towards finding self-identity. It grasps nature, reifies it and conceals its depth. Consciousness wants to be whole, but it easily trades this for totalitarian centralism, for a dummy consciousness. For this reason, Heraclitus warns us that the unity of knowledge is different, that the world does not have to be centrally steered: "The wise is one, knowing the plan by which it steers (*kybernesthai*) all things through all."[55]

And why does nature like to hide? So that we do not fear its abyss. Perhaps also so that we can know it in a way that opens up practical applications as well. In this, *physis* enables its beauty to not always be terrifying, and enables also all of the dullness and beauty of philosophy and science. It hides partly in order for actuality to be alive and capable of surprising us, even in spite of all our efforts at gaining knowledge.

---

55   Heraclitus B41. Kahn, *Art*, 55.

About the author . . .

Zdeněk Kratochvíl was born in 1952. Since 1990 he has been lecturing in both the Department of Philosophy and the History of Natural Sciences in the Natural Sciences Faculty at the Charles University and at the Institute of Philosophic and Religious Studies in the Faculty of Philosophy at the Charles University. His primary interests lie with the relation between philosophy and non-philosophy, both in the historical sense and the topical one. In particular, he's interested in the proto-philosophical thinking of archaic Greece (the pre-Socratics, especially Heraclitus) and the relationship between this thinking and the religion of Ancient Greece, with emergent science and with transformations in art. He's also interested in current questions of the relations between philosophy, science, and religion, and chiefly with the philosophy of nature.

From his publications

Mýtus, filosofie a věda (Prague: Karolinum, 1991).
Filosofie živé přírody (Prague: Herrmann a synové, 1994).
Od mýtu k logu (Prague: Herrmann a synové, 1994), 45–175.
Řeč umění a archaické filosofie (Prague: Herrmann a synové, 1995), 129–251.
Obrana želvy (Prague: Malvern, 2003).
Délský potápěč k Hérakleitově řeči (Prague: Herrmann a synové, 2006).
Filosofie mezi mýtem a vědou (od Homéra po Descarta) (Prague: Academia, 2009).
A. Markoš et al., *Life as Its Own Designer (Darwin's Origin and Western Thought)* (Heidelberg, 2009).
Mezi mořem a nebem. Odkaz archaické vnímavosti (Červený Kostelec: Pavel Mervart, 2010).
Anaxagorás (Červený Kostelec: Pavel Mervart, 2014).

He manages a private Czech language internet domain (fysis.cz) and runs the Greek part of the Anglophone university database for the pictorial documentation of the Greek religion on Wikimedia Commons (https://commons.wikimedia.org/wiki/User:Zde).